Transportation Theme-A-Saurus

The Great Big Book of Things on the Move

By THE TOTLINE STAFF

Illustrated by GARY MOHRMAN

Totline® Publications
A Division of Frank Schaffer Publications, Inc.
Torrance, California

Editors: Kathleen Cubley and Carol Gnojewski
Contributing Editors: Durby Peterson and Jean Warren
Proofreader: Kris Fulsaas
Graphic Designer (Interior): Sarah Ness
Graphic Designer (Cover): Brenda Mann Harrison
Illustrator (Cover): Kathy Kotomaimoce
Production Manager: Melody Olney

ISBN 1-57029-264-7

Printed in the United States of America
Published by Totline® Publications
23740 Hawthorne Blvd.
Torrance, CA 90505

Introduction

Transportation Theme-A-Saurus is designed as a resource for helping young children explore transportation systems. The book is filled with easy hands-on activities that invite children to learn about everyday vehicles in creative and informative ways.

Each unit contains a collection of activities from a variety of curriculum areas such as art, science, language, learning games, movement, music, and snacks. Some units contain ideas for extending activities into longer group projects using the project approach method. All of the ideas in this book are developmentally appropriate for preschoolers, and use only inexpensive, readily available materials.

Transportation systems are all around children and impact their lives on a daily basis. As you work with the units in this book, you will find that opportunities for teaching about transportation are everywhere. Feel free to take advantage of these opportunities, incorporating your own ideas and heightening your awareness of these systems as you encourage your children to learn more about the vehicles they know and to find out about new ones. Let *Transportation Theme-A-Saurus* transform learning into an adventure filled with fun and discovery.

Contents

On the Road

In the Air

On Water

On Tracks

On Snow

On the Road

Bikes & Trikes

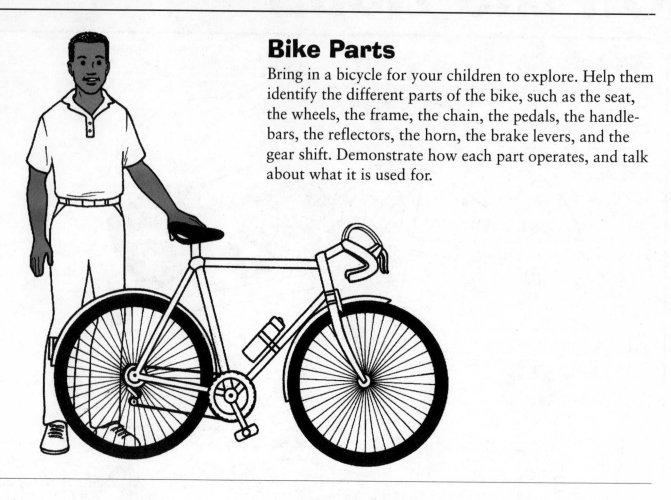

Bike Parts

Bring in a bicycle for your children to explore. Help them identify the different parts of the bike, such as the seat, the wheels, the frame, the chain, the pedals, the handlebars, the reflectors, the horn, the brake levers, and the gear shift. Demonstrate how each part operates, and talk about what it is used for.

Bike Makers

After reviewing the parts of a bicycle, let your children put together their own bikes. Using the Bike Puzzle Pattern on page 15 as a guide, cut bike parts out of felt. Then invite the children to arrange the pieces on a flannelboard any way they choose. Encourage them to name their bike creations and talk about how they work.

Cycle Song

Sung to: "The Farmer in the Dell"

My cycle has two wheels.

My cycle has two wheels.

It is called a bicycle.

My cycle with two wheels.

Substitute other numbers in place of *two*. Have the children name or make up names for cycles with different numbers of wheels: one wheel (unicycle), three wheels (tricycle).

Carol Gnojewski

Bike Maintenance

Just like cars, bikes need to be checked and fixed routinely to make sure that their parts are working correctly. Tires need to be checked for air and wear. Chains need to be oiled and brakes need to be adjusted. Handlebars and seats need to be repositioned as the children grow.

If possible, invite a repair person from your local bike shop to visit your group. Or ask a parent or staff member who is adept at fixing bikes. Invite the bike repair person to talk about his or her job. With permission, have him or her demonstrate how to fix a bike and check your facility's bikes, trikes, and riding vehicles for minor repairs and adjustments. Encourage the children to watch and help.

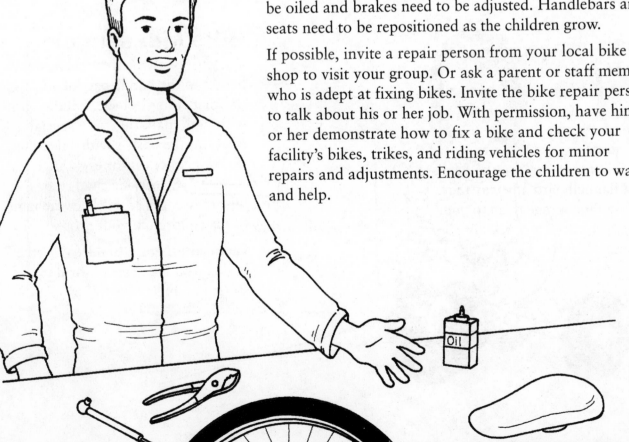

Cycle Stretch

Gather your children in a circle. Invite them to spread out and then lie down with their back on the floor and their arms to their sides. Have them lift their legs into the air. Show them how to move their legs in circles as if they were pedaling a bike. If you wish, have them raise their arms and grip pretend handlebars.

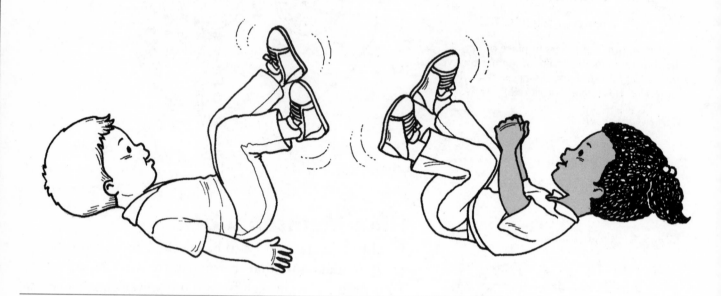

Bike Messenger

Use yarn or twine to attach a small basket to the handlebars of a tricycle or other riding vehicle. Fill the basket with junk mail. (Or for a special treat, fill the basket with valentines, candy, or stickers for each of your children.) Select one child to be the bike messenger and deliver the mail to the children in your group.

Variation: Let the children use the basket as a bike carrier for dolls or stuffed animals.

Bike Trail

Use chalk, blocks, or tape to mark off a bike trail through your room or play yard. Try to make it in a place that is out of the way of the normal path of play. Decide as a group which direction the children should steer their riding vehicles in to prevent collisions. Make sure that they wear their bike helmets when they ride.

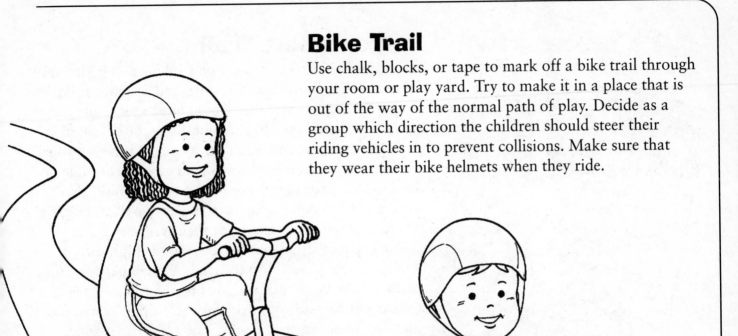

Foot Crank

Turn a tricycle upside down so that the pedals of the front wheel are in the air. Show your children how to turn the pedals with their hands to make the front wheel turn. Explain that the pedals and wheel combine to make a device called a crank. Other common crank devices include egg beaters, pencil sharpeners, and old-fashioned ice cream churns. If you wish, invite the children to pretend that the tricycle pedal is an ice cream crank, and that they are churning pretend ice cream. As they turn the crank, have each child decide which flavor of ice cream they are making.

Extension: Bring in child-safe crank machines, such as a real ice cream churn, for your children to explore.

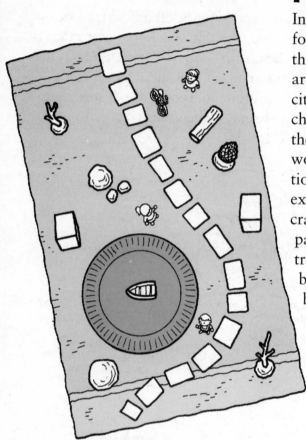

Pretend Bike Trail

Invite your children to make a play biking and hiking trail for their small plastic bikes, people, and animals. Have them think about what they would like to see while they are riding. Would they like to bike along the beach, in a city, near a playground, or in the woods? Then give your children a large green or brown bath towel to arrange on the floor for a base (green or brown fabric would also work well). Encourage your children to use their imagination to come up with details for their trail scene. For example, paper strips, thin blocks, wood chips, dirt, or craft sticks could mark off the trail. A small paper plate painted blue would make a great pond or lake. Pretend trees could be made by sticking twigs or pine cones into balls of modeling clay. Rocks, wood blocks, or small boxes would make nice houses, skyscrapers, or other city buildings.

Speed Sign Sequence

On roads, speed signs tell drivers how fast they can drive to be safe. Explain that high numbers mean you can drive fast and low numbers mean you need to drive more slowly. From a set of blank index cards, make a set of five speed limit signs. Number the signs from 1 to 5. Staple each sign to a plastic drinking straw. Poke each straw into a lump of modeling clay. Then place the signs at various points alongside your bike trail. As the children ride around the trail, have them drive faster or slower as the speed signs dictate.

Variation: Challenge the children to arrange the signs in order from the slowest speed limit to the highest speed limit, or vice versa.

Doll Bike Helmets

Save old whipped-topping containers. Turn them upside-down. Let your children cover them with stickers and put them on the head of dolls and stuffed animals for Doll Bike Helmets. Help the children strap their dolls or stuffed animals onto their riding vehicles and give them a ride.

Hint: Use dolls, stuffed animals, or puppets wearing helmets when you want to reinforce tricycle and bicycle safety.

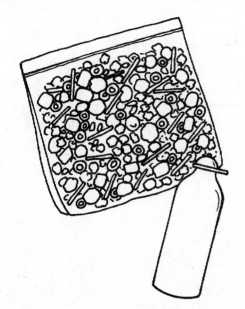

Trail Mix

Pour any of the following ingredients into a large resealable plastic bag. Let your children help you shake the bag to mix. Then divide the trail mix into child-size portions for your hungry riders. Provide the children with water bottles filled with water or juice to wash down their snack.

Dried fruit

Fish-shaped crackers

Flaked coconut

Granola

Nuts

O-shaped cereal pieces

Pretzel sticks

Rice crackers

Sesame sticks

Small chocolate candies

Sunflower seeds

Bike Registration

Explain to your children that a bicycle license is similar to a license plate on a car. It can help police officers find your bike if it is lost or stolen. Contact your local city hall or police station for information about bike registration. If possible, register the bikes and trikes in your facility, and show your children what a bicycle license looks like. Pass on information about your city's bicycle registration process to the parents of your children through a bulletin board or newsletter.

Extension: If you wish, bring in some old car license plates for the children to examine. Spread newsprint over the license plates and let them use crayons or chalk to make license plate rubbings.

Photo Drivers License

Let each of your children make a photo drivers license to use when they drive the riding vehicles in your facility. Have them glue photographs of themselves onto index cards. On the back of the card, help each child write or trace a sentence that says: (Child's name) knows bike safety rules." If you wish, laminate the licenses with clear self-stick paper.

Bike Puzzle Pattern

Use with the activity on page 8.

Bridges

Walking Bridge

To build an indoor-outdoor walking bridge for your children to enjoy, you will need eight cinder building blocks (found at hardware, lumber, and building supply stores) and one 8-foot wooden plank that has been sanded smooth. Stack four cinder blocks (two blocks high by two blocks wide) under each end of the walking plank. Be sure that the holes in the cinder blocks are all facing upward.

Caution: Children will want to jump off the bridge, so stay close by to assist with bridge walking and to supervise jumping. Younger children may need extra help climbing up onto the bridge.

Over and Under

Vehicles travel both over and under bridges. Talk about vehicles that travel under bridges, such as boats, and vehicles that travel over bridges, such as cars and trains. As you supervise play on the Walking Bridge, sing the song "Over the Bridge." Give each child the option of walking over or crawling under your bridge.

Over the Bridge

Sung to: "The Bear Went Over the Mountain"

The bridge goes over the water,

The bridge goes over the water,

The bridge goes over the water,

And I go over the bridge.

Additional verses: The train goes over the bridge; The boat goes under the bridge; The car goes over the bridge; The car goes under the bridge.

Substitute *under* for *over*, depending on your children's actions.

Carol Gnojewski

Water Table Bridge

Span the waters of your water table with this simple bridge. Select a large piece of vinyl (a discarded tablecloth or shower curtain works well). With a heavy pair of scissors, cut a 5-inch-wide strip of vinyl that is about 8 inches longer than the widest part of your water table. Stretch the vinyl strip from one side of the water table to the other, and secure it to the sides of the table with duct tape. Children will love helping plastic action figures and animals cross the bridge and dive into the water.

Shimmering Bridge Mural

Draw the rough outline of a large suspension bridge on butcher paper. Offer your children a gold or silver metallic stamp pad. Have them press their fingertips onto the stamp pad and then onto the bridge outline to make a shimmering bridge. Attach the completed bridge mural to a wall at the children's eye level.

Hint: Clean the children's fingers with rubber stamp cleaner or window cleaner. Have the children wash their hands with soap and water after the ink is gone.

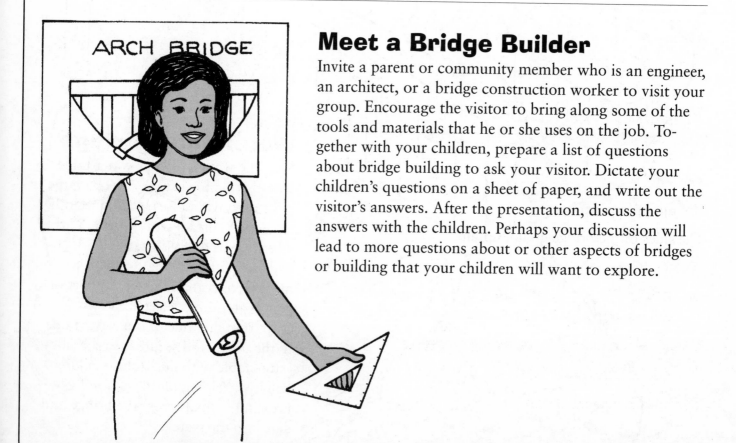

Meet a Bridge Builder

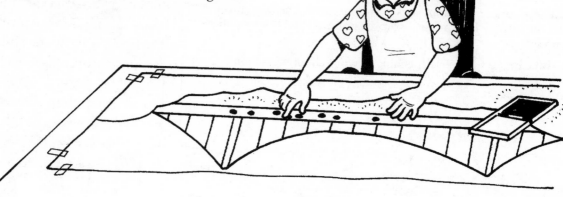

Invite a parent or community member who is an engineer, an architect, or a bridge construction worker to visit your group. Encourage the visitor to bring along some of the tools and materials that he or she uses on the job. Together with your children, prepare a list of questions about bridge building to ask your visitor. Dictate your children's questions on a sheet of paper, and write out the visitor's answers. After the presentation, discuss the answers with the children. Perhaps your discussion will lead to more questions about or other aspects of bridges or building that your children will want to explore.

The Drawbridge

Sung to: "The Wheels on the Bus"

The sides of the bridge go up, up, up;

Up, up, up; up, up up.

The sides of the bridge go up, up, up

When a boat wants to pass.

The sides of the bridge go down, down, down;

Down, down, down; down, down, down.

The sides of the bridge go down, down, down—

The boat is through at last!

Jean Warren

Drawbridge Game

Talk to your children about draw-bridges and how they work. Have any of your children ever seen a draw-bridge? What did it do? If possible, show them a picture of a drawbridge or, even better, a toy drawbridge from a construction set. Then have your children choose partners. Demonstrate for the pairs how to stand facing one another, with arms extended and palms touching, to portray a flat drawbridge. Show the children how to raise their arms to allow ships to pass underneath. Assign some of your children to be the drawbridges and others to be tall ships passing through the drawbridges. Be sure that everyone has a turn to be both a drawbridge and a tall ship.

Extension: Sing "The Drawbridge" as you play.

Tollbooth

Set up a tollbooth change catcher next to any of your favorite bridge-crossing activities. To make a change catcher, use duct tape to attach a plastic bucket to a wall or sturdy piece of furniture. Label the bucket "5 cents" or "10 cents." Provide play money for your children to toss into the change catcher before crossing the bridge.

Building Bridges

Help your children turn an empty shoebox into a bridge for toy cars. Turn the box upside down and cut open the corner seams at both ends to create ramps for cars to drive over. Trim the two long sides and then cut semicircles, as shown in the illustration. Have the children use markers or stickers to decorate the outside of the bridge.

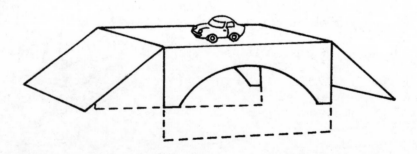

Bridges to Eat

Snack on these tasty bridges. Give each of your children four thin pretzel sticks and four jumbo marshmallows. Poke a pretzel stick into each marshmallow. These will be drawbridge supports. Rest one whole graham cracker on top of the pretzel sticks. Eat and enjoy.

Many Bridges

There are many types of bridges. Most are constructed over water, while some span canyons or cross over train tracks and roadways. Modern bridges are made out of steel, but some existing bridges are made from stone and wood. Some wooden bridges even have coverings over them.

Bring in metal, stone, and wood items for your children to explore.

Extension: Provide your children with books about bridges. Keep these books in your block or construction areas, as well as your reading areas, to give children bridge-building ideas.

Buses

Parts of a Bus

Children love buses, and they enjoy learning about the parts of a bus. Have your children help you think of some of the parts of a bus, such as the steering wheel, the wheels, and the headlights, the seats, the doors, the buzzer you pull when you want to get off the bus. Have any of your children been on a bus? What did they like about their ride? What didn't they like? Do they remember where they went?

Wheels on the Bus

For each of your children draw one or two simple bus shapes on pieces of construction paper (or photocopy bus shapes onto construction paper). Give each child two to four black wheels and some glue. Let the children attach the wheels to the bus shapes. If desired, let your children sing "The Wheels on the Bus" (on this page) while doing this activity.

The Wheels on the Bus

The wheels on the bus go round and round,

Round and round, round and round.

The wheels on the bus go round and round

All over town.

Additional verses: The people on the bus go chit, chit, chat; The babies on the bus go waa, waa, waa; The wipers on the bus go swish, swish, swish; The lights on the bus go off and on; The horn on the bus goes honk, honk, honk.

Adapted Traditional

Bus Driver

Bus driver, bus driver, may I have a ride?
(Hold up fist and wiggle thumb.)

Yes, yes, please step inside.
(Hold up other fist and wiggle thumb.)

Put in some money.
(Bend down first thumb.)

Step on the gas.
(Bend down other thumb.)

Chug-a-way, chug-a-way,
(Pretend to steer bus.)

But not too fast.

Adapted Traditional

Bus Fares

Set up two rows of chairs, one for each of your children, plus one for the bus driver. Set a container, such as a round oatmeal container, next to the driver seat. Give each of your children a toy coin. Have them line up while you sit in the driver's seat. As your children get on the "bus," have them drop their fare into the container. When everyone is one the bus, take a little trip.

Bus Routes

City buses have fixed routes. They travel on the same roads and make the same stops every day. This helps people decide which bus will take them where they need to go. Identify the fixed routes in your facility. Which are the normal routes you take as a group to travel to the play yard? The snack area? The bathroom? If possible, help your children discover new ways to get to different parts of your room and facility.

Traveling Billboards

Most city bus systems and some bus lines such as Greyhound paint the sides of their buses for ads or promotions. These buses become traveling billboards, read by commuters and passersby.

Show your children pictures of billboards or take a field trip to see one. Read the billboards to your children. Talk about how the words and pictures capture your attention. Together, design a billboard to advertise your facility or group.

Tour Bus

Taking a ride on a tour bus is a fun way to learn more about a city you are visiting. In these special buses, a tour guide stands at the front of the bus and points out interesting things to see out the window, such as buildings, parks, and statues. Sometimes the tour guide will tell funny stories about the things that you see.

Have your children pretend that they are on a tour bus. Pick one child to be the bus driver, and one to be the tour guide who takes the class on a tour around your room.

Double Decker

A double-decker bus has two levels for people to ride in. This is because *double* means "two." To get to the top level, you have to climb stairs. Riding at the top of a double-decker bus gives you a better view, because you are up higher and can see farther.

Discuss *single* and *double* with your children. Then ask your children which can carry more people, a double-decker bus or a regular city bus? Experiment with single and double by setting out rows of flat objects such as blocks, poker chips, cans, lids, and plates. Have the children make them double by stacking another layer on top.

Variation: Direct each child to make a single or a double row of objects.

Double-Decker Treats

At snacktime, help your children make double-decker hors d'oeuvres by layering crackers, vegetables, meat, cheese, or fruit.

Extension: Take a field trip to your local ice cream parlor. Order single, double-decker, and double-dipped cones so your children can see how they are made, and what they look like. If you wish, set up an ice cream parlor in your dramatic play area. Provide the children with modeling dough for making single and double-decker servings.

Group Bus

Cut a large school bus shape out of butcher paper and have your children work together to paint it yellow. Make the bus large enough to draw in a 6½-inch window for each child. When it is dry, tape the bus to a wall in your room.

Then provide the children with plain, 6-inch paper plates and a variety of collage materials including yarn and paper scraps. Encourage each child to use the collage materials to make a facial self-portrait. Tape the paper plate portraits in the windows of the bus for a group mural.

Hint: Older preschoolers may want to draw pictures of themselves on plain white paper.

Variation: Instead of making portraits, have each of your children bring in a photo from home. Or take candid photos of your children using an instant camera.

School Bus Yellow

Today, school buses are readily recognized by their bright yellow color. But it wasn't until 1939 that national school-bus standards were developed and yellow became the official "National School Bus Chrome." The bright orange-yellow color was selected because the black school bus lettering shows up the best in this hue and can be seen in the early morning hours when children are picked up for school.

Give each of your children a piece of yellow construction paper and black paint. Have them use the black paint to write or make marks on the paper. Then have them paint black marks on other construction paper colors. When they are dry, display the paintings in a darkened corner of your room. Compare the colors. On which colors does the black paint show up the best?

School Bus Safety

The third full week of October is National School Bus Safety Week. This is a good week to review safe bus riding behavior with your children. If possible, take your children on a real bus ride. Or set up rows of chairs in your classroom as a pretend bus and practice boarding, riding, and exiting. Point out the "danger zone" in the front and back of the bus. A bus driver may not see you if you stay in these areas after leaving the bus. Remind your children that cars are supposed to stop while the red stop arm is out, but they need to watch out for cars just in case. The following are a few important bus safety rules.

🚌 Stay off the street while you wait for the bus.

🚌 Wait to board the bus until it is completely stopped and the driver has opened the door.

🚌 Stay seated at all times.

🚌 Keep hands inside the bus and to yourself.

🚌 Keep your belongings next to you on the seat.

🚌 Leave your seat only to exit when the bus has completely stopped.

🚌 Use the handrail to step off the bus.

🚌 Take giant steps away from the bus and toward the sidewalk.

🚌 If you must cross the street, cross in front of the bus. Make sure that the driver sees you. The bus driver may not see you if you cross behind the bus.

🚌 If you forget something on a bus, tell a parent or teacher. Don't run back to retrieve items that are dropped or forgotten.

Hint: For more information about National School Bus Safety Week, write to the National School Transportation Association (NSTA), P.O. Box 2639, Springfield, VA 22152.

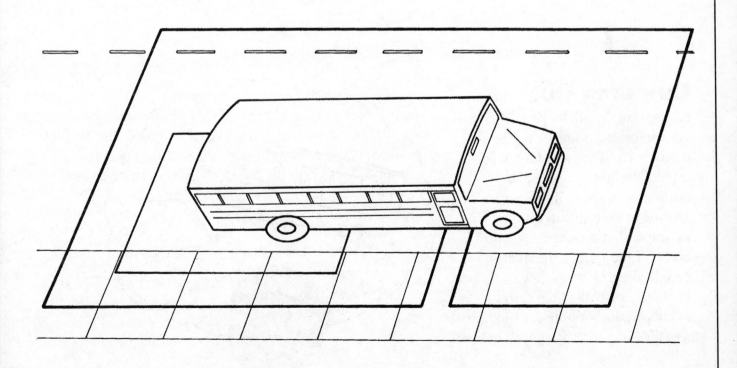

Campers

Homes on Wheels

Explain to your children that campers and motor homes are like miniature homes on wheels. *Campers* are trucks with compartments attached to the back of them that have space for sleeping and eating. *Motor homes* have built-in spaces for sleeping and eating. Bring in pictures of these types of vehicles. (Your local RV dealer should have full-color brochures or catalogs that show the inside and outside of different camper and motor home models.)

Then photocopy the RV pattern on page 31 and cover it with clear self-stick paper. Talk with the children about the areas in the motor home that correspond with the rooms that they have in their homes. Have them cut, from magazines and catalogs, pictures of items that can be found in various rooms of their homes. Let the children sort the items they have cut into four piles: things that belong in the kitchen, things that belong in the bedroom, things that belong in the bathroom, and things that belong in the living room. Have them place these items in the corresponding areas of the motor home.

Camping Out

Recreational vehicles such as campers and motor homes are primarily used for camping and for vacation travel. Discuss camping and vacationing with your children. Has anyone in your group camped or vacationed in a camper or motor home? Talk about other places people sleep in when they camp or vacation, such as in tents, in lodges or cabins, and in hotels. Compare what it's like to "camp out" in these different ways.

Abbreviated Letter Fun

Recreational vehicles are called RVs. This is an abbreviation, or shortened form, of *recreational vehicle* made by using the first letter of each word. Common abbreviations that your children might know include PJs, TV, CD, and VCR. What are the long forms of these names?

Provide the children with magnetic letters and a magnetic surface such as a baking sheet. Let them use the letters to create their own real or make-believe abbreviated words.

Trailer Discovery

Bring in an adult-size bicycle and a child-size bicycle trailer for your children to explore. Show the children how to hook the trailer up to the back of the bicycle. Explain that this process is similar to how a trailer is attached to the back of a truck. If you wish, let one or two children at a time climb inside the trailer. Give the children rides around your play yard.

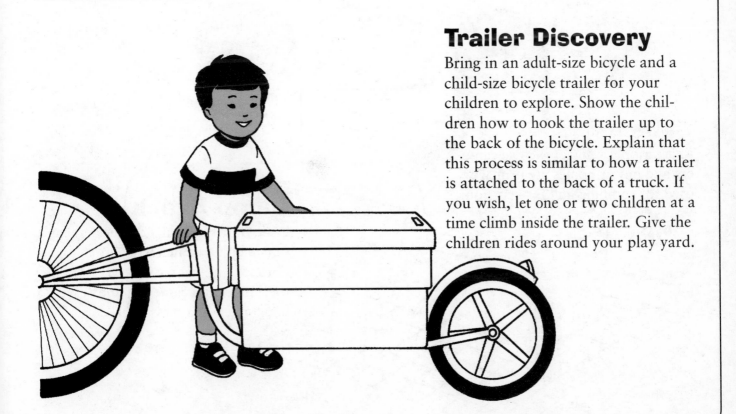

Group Camping Trip

Contact your state's parks and recreation office for informational literature, maps, and brochures about local campgrounds and campsites. Find out which sites have hookups for campers and motor homes.

Then invite your children to plan a pretend trip to one of these sites. Encourage them to make up a list of supplies and equipment they will need. Guide their thinking with questions such as, "How many days do you want to camp? What fun things do you want to do on the trip (fish, hike, boat, or play other sports and games)? What types of supplies or equipment are already available at the campsite?"

Extension: If you wish, set up a campsite in your room. Ask parents to donate old camping equipment and clothing, such as blankets, sleeping bags, flashlights, backpacks, camp stools, and cooking utensils. Plan fun camping activities such as telling camp stories, singing camp songs, and taking a hike through your room or play yard.

Camp Snack

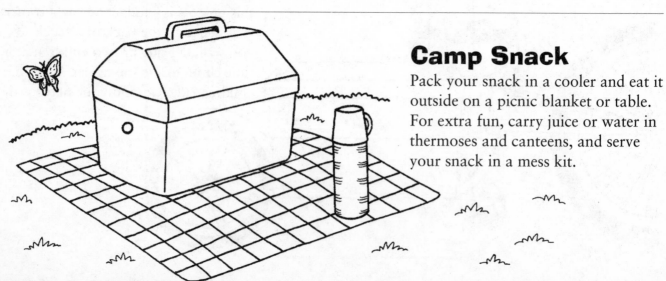

Pack your snack in a cooler and eat it outside on a picnic blanket or table. For extra fun, carry juice or water in thermoses and canteens, and serve your snack in a mess kit.

RV Pattern

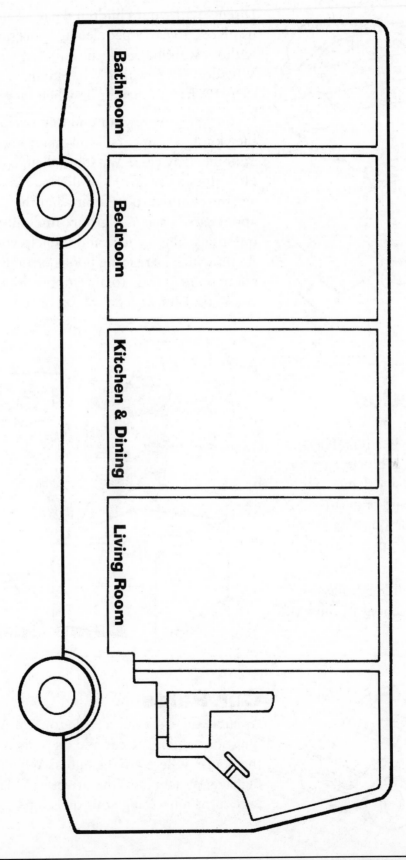

Bathroom

Bedroom

Kitchen & Dining

Living Room

Cars

Cars Help Us

Discuss with your children what we use cars for (to take us places, to carry people and groceries, to get somewhere without walking). Ask the children where they go in cars. Why don't they walk? What kinds of things can cars carry? What do they bring when they go on a car trip?

If you wish, invite your children to share with you what they know about cars. How many children have real cars at home? Toy cars? What are their favorite kinds of cars? How does a car go? How do you make it stop? Encourage the children to tell you what they would like to know about cars. Then as a group, find out the answers to their questions. Have your children help you think of ways to do this, such as reading books or magazines about cars, going on field trips to automobile lots, or bringing in guest speakers who drive, fix, or sell cars.

Car Collection

Collect all of the small toy cars in your room and put them in a box. Have your children use this box of cars for sorting and matching activities. This could work as a group or partner project or for one-on-one play. Afterward, let the children play with the toy cars.

Variation: Have children bring in a car or their car collections to show to your group.

Car Parts

At circle time, set out a large toy car. Ask the children questions about the car and its parts, such as, "Where is the hood? Where are the lights? Where would you put luggage? Where does the driver sit?" Have the children take turns answering your questions.

Car Numbers

Give each of your children a toy car, such as a matchbox car, or a picture of a car (cut from an auto magazine). Ask your children to tell you how many wheels their car has by holding up that many fingers. In this manner, have the children find out how many lights, seats, steering wheels, and doors are on their vehicle.

Extension: If you wish, use the data from this activity to make a graph about cars for your children. Talk about your findings.

Car Noises

Make a tape of car sounds, including the sounds of a blinker, a windshield wiper, a horn, and an engine starting or turning over. Play this tape to your group and talk about each sound. Can your children identify these car noises? Talk about some other sounds cars make, especially when they need to be repaired. If you wish, invite your children to develop motions, such as swiping their arms back and forth when they hear the windshield wiper noise, for each car sound.

Start and Stop Game

Have your children line up in a horizontal line across the room. Stand in front of them with a paper plate. Invite them to pretend that you are the car driver and the paper plate is the steering wheel. Explain that a steering wheel is connected to the front wheels and makes them change directions. Show them that if you turn the steering wheel one way the wheels turn that way, too. If you turn the wheel the other way, the wheels will follow. Then have the children pretend to be the front wheels of your car. Using the steering wheel, direct the children to turn from side to side. Encourage them to watch and move with you as you turn the steering wheel this way and that. When you want the children to stop, press down as if you're putting on the brake. Give older preschoolers the opportunity to be the driver and take the wheel.

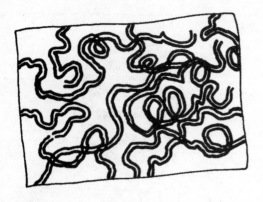

Car Tracks

Cover a large table with newsprint or butcher paper. Place on the paper several shallow containers of tempera paint in various colors. Set out enough small plastic cars for each of your children to have one. Invite your children to dip the wheels of their cars into the paint and then drive them around on the paper to leave tire tracks. Afterward, have them step back and look at where their cars have been. Are there different types of tracks?

Family Car Puzzles

Cut pictures of various types of family cars from magazines. Try to include station wagons, hatchbacks, mini-vans, and sedans. Mount each picture on heavy paper and cover both sides with clear self-stick paper. Cut out the car shapes and then cut each one into several puzzle pieces. Place each puzzle in a separate resealable plastic bag and give them to your children to put together. Increase the challenge by mixing up the pieces from two or three puzzles and letting your children sort out the pieces to complete each puzzle.

Cars in the Garage

Select a large, shallow box with the top flaps removed. Cut a wide doorway in one side to make a parking garage. Find a number of different-colored toy cars. On the floor of the garage, draw rectangles that match the colors of the toy cars. Your children will enjoy taking turns driving the cars into the garage and then parking them in the matching-colored "parking space."

Variation: Write numerals in the parking spaces. Use masking tape to label the cars with matching numbers. As the children drive their toy cars up to the garage, let one child at a time be the parking garage attendant who tells the drivers which space is theirs.

Ride-Along Game

Invite your children to stand together as a group in the center of an open area. As you teach them to sing "What a Ride," take the hand of one child and walk together around the group. Then for the next verse, have that child take the hand of another child from the center and all three of you take a lap around the group again. Continue singing and walking around the group, adding one more child as you sing each verse. When all the children are holding hands, sing the last verse and take another lap around the room together, with everyone bumping up and down and side to side as you go.

What a Ride

Sung to: "The Farmer in the Dell"

Our family took a ride,

Our family took a ride.

Bumpety-bumping side to side,

Our family took a ride.

We also brought our friend,

We also brought our friend.

Bumpety-bumping side to side,

Our family took a ride.

We also brought our dog,

We also brought our dog.

Bumpety-bumping side to side,

Our family took a ride.

Additional verses: We also brought our cousin, our aunt, our uncle, etc.

Last verse:

Oh, what a ride,

Oh, what a ride.

Bumpety-bumping side to side,

Our family took a ride.

Durby Peterson

Limousine Luxury

Explain to your children that a limousine is an extra long and fancy car driven by a hired driver, called a chauffeur. (Show a picture, if possible.) Limousines come with special features, such as a TV, a sun roof, dark windows, luxurious seats, and sometimes a divider between the chauffeur and the back seat for privacy. People such as kings, queens, and presidents ride in limousines. Other people can rent limousines for special occasions such as weddings. Help your children make a "limousine" by arranging chairs so there is a large distance between the driver's seat and the back seat. Let your children dress up and take turns chauffeuring each other to special places.

Come See the Parade!

Many people decorate their cars for parades. Ask your children how they would decorate a car for a parade. Make a list on butcher paper of what they would need to decorate their car. Set out some of the decoration materials you have on hand (streamers, balloons, etc.) and let your children decorate a few trikes. Then let them parade the trikes around the play yard.

The Joyful Jeep

Help your children compare sizes with this flannelboard activity. Cut from brown felt a speedbump-sized hill, a bigger hill, and a large mountain. Then cut from green felt a simple jeep, as shown in the illustration. As you recite the first verse of the rhyme "Our Jeep," place the hills on the flannelboard one at a time, from left to right. During verses two and three, move the jeep over the hills, reversing direction once it gets to the mountaintop. Talk with your children about which hill is small, medium, and large. Let your children take turns moving the jeep as you all recite the rhyme again.

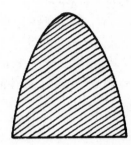

Dune Buggy Day

Show your children a picture of a dune buggy. Explain that a dune buggy is a lightweight car that is specially designed to travel over sand. Although most cars would get stuck in the sand, dune buggies ride low to the ground and have wide, soft tires that give them plenty of traction. Set out some toy cars by the sandbox. Your children will enjoy piling up sand and then pretending the cars are dune buggies driving over enormous dunes.

Our Jeep

First we saw a bump,

Then we saw a hill,

Then we saw a mountain

That was bigger, still.

Our jeep drove over the bump,

Our jeep drove over the hill,

Our jeep drove up the mountain

And it's up there, still.

Let's drive back down the mountain,

Let's drive back over the hill,

Let's drive back over the bump.

Then let's just sit still!

Durby Peterson

Sports Cars

If possible, locate a brochure from a sports car dealership and show the pictures to your children. Point out the low, sleek designs and bold colors. Talk about the special features such as winker headlights, roll bars, wing spoilers, etc.

Let your children design their own sports cars. Set out a variety of large facial-tissue boxes, construction paper, scissors, felt-tip marker, and tape. Help your children add round construction paper wheels to the sides of their cars. They might add a cardboard windshield, headlights, and a spoiler on the back. Talk about the importance of buckling up and driving safely.

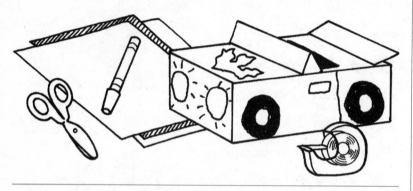

Fun on the Road

Using duct or masking tape, connect two large pieces of posterboard to make a large road map on the floor. Pencil in some roads that curve through the countryside and intersect in towns. When you get the layout right, use markers to outline the roads in black with yellow centerline stripes. Add more color with trees, lakes, and stop signs. Set out a variety of small toy sports cars and invite your children to take them for a drive on the map.

My Little Sports Car

Sung to: "Camptown Races"

Hop aboard my little sports car.

Vroom, vroom! Beep, beep!

Hop aboard my little sports car.

Let's take it down the road.

Chorus:

Zipping as we go,

Zooming fast or slow,

Hop aboard my little sports car.

Let's take it down the road.

My sports car is shiny red.

Vroom, vroom! Beep, beep!

Safely watching out ahead,

Let's take it down the road.

Chorus

Jean Warren

Old and New

Check your library for illustrated books of old-time cars such as *The Model T Ford*, by Christopher Simonds (Silver-Burdett, 1991). Old-time cars, such as Model Ts, had a handle, called a crank, in the front that the driver turned to start the car. What do we use to start cars today? Provide your children with pictures or models of modern cars to help compare them with old-time cars. What are some other differences they notice?

Extension: Bring in keys and padlocks for your children to play with. Show them how to turn the keys different ways to lock and unlock the padlocks. Explain that this turning motion is similar to how you unlock a steering column and start the engine on a car. Keep keys in your home-life area for the children to use when they pretend to drive cars.

Model T Tune

Sung to: "Row, Row, Row, Your Boat"

Turn, turn, turn the crank
  (Pretend to turn crank.)

On your Model T.

When the motor loudly hums,

Hop inside with me.
  (Sit on a chair.)

Steer, steer, steer the wheel
  (Make steering motions.)

On your Model T.

Down the road we'll bump along,
  (Bump up and down.)

Think of all we'll see!
  (Point to imaginary sites.)

Durby Peterson

What Car Am I?

Sung to: "London Bridge"

I'm a car from long ago,

I am black, I go slow.

Turn a crank to make me go.

What car am I?
(*Model T*)

I take families for a ride.

Lots of seats are inside,

Big windows on every side.

What car am I?
(*Minivan*)

I drive you around the town.

Hop on in, sit right down.

Tell me where to take you 'round.

What car am I?
(*Taxi-cab*)

I have little room inside

But I'm still quite a ride.

Hold on, as I zoom and slide

What car am I?
(*Sports car*)

I am sturdy and I'm tough.

I climb hills that are rough.

My four wheels all grip enough.

What car am I?
(*Jeep or Land Rover*)

Durby Peterson

Car Cards

Using the patterns on pages 42 and 43, make a car card for each child in your group. (You may have to make identical cards for some of the children.) After each verse of the song "What Car Am I?" let the children call out the name of the car described and have the children with the appropriate cards hold them up.

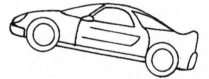

Have Box, Will Travel

Create a place where your children can pretend to take a road trip without leaving the room. Place some large, wide boxes together on the floor so that one or two children can sit in each box. Let your children help create their cars by finding scraps of cardboard for the license plates, a paper plate for the steering wheel, and some stuffed animal friends for company. Let them take turns being the driver and the passengers. Suggest the following travel games for their trip.

Color-Coded Fun

Give the "driver" a small assortment of colored blocks or other small objects. Have him or her pick up a green block and say, "Green, green, I see something green." The driver then looks out the "window" (around the room) and names something that is green before passing the colored block to the next person. The game continues until everyone has named something green. Then another child selects a different-colored block and starts the game again, looking for things that match the new block. Continue play until each child has selected a block and passed it around.

Multi-Car Mural

Collect pictures of as many different types of cars as you can. You might look in magazines, or photocopy pictures from books. Try to include pictures of sports cars, limousines, taxi-cabs, minivans, station wagons, jeeps, and a Model T, if possible. Cut around each car and set the pictures on a table. Invite your children to make a mural by gluing the pictures all over a large white posterboard. Afterward, talk with your children about all the different types and colors they see. How are the cars different from each other? How are they alike? Which ones do your children like best?

Car Patterns

Use with activity on page 40.

Car Patterns

Use with activity on page 40.

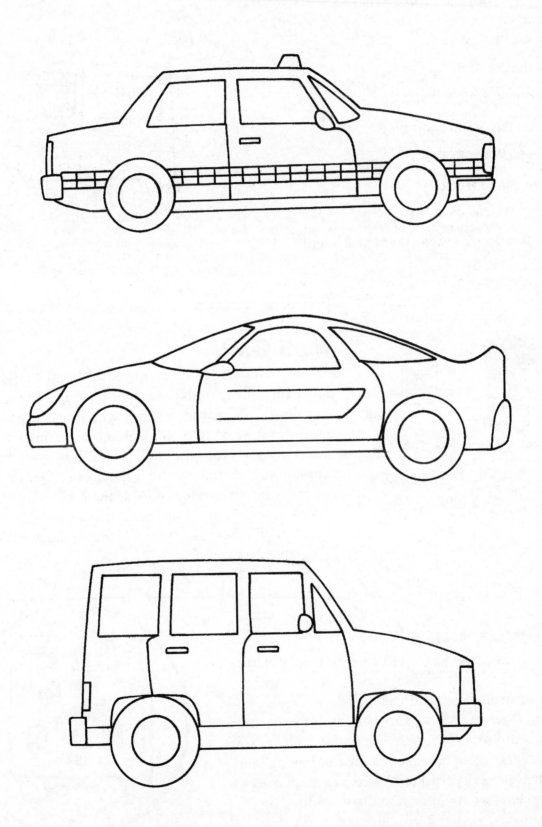

Community Service Vehicles

I Can Drive a Mail Truck

Sung to: "Do Your Ears Hang Low?"

I can drive a mail truck

Through the snow and rain and muck

To deliver mail, over hill and dale.

In my truck red, white, and blue

Are some packages for you.

I can drive a mail truck.

Repeat, substituting *letters, boxes, post cards,* or *parcels* for *packages.* Invite your children to think of other items mail carriers deliver. What is the best thing they have ever received by mail?

Diane Thom

Mail Call

Write the numeral 1 on an index card and a large envelope. Tape the card to the front of a coffee can to make a "mailbox." Repeat the process with successive numerals until you have 5–10 mailboxes and matching envelopes. Select a wagon (or other pull toy) to be the mail truck. Explain to your children that the mail carrier drives around putting envelopes inside the mailbox with a matching number. Dump the envelopes into the wagon. Let your children take turns delivering the mail. Sing the song above as you play.

Mail Truck Snack

Place a large slice of wheat bread on each child's plate. Trim off the crust and then cut away one corner so it resembles the front of a mail truck, as shown in the illustration. Place two round slices of carrot or cucumber below the bread for the wheels. Then place a pile of small square crackers on the bread. Let your children pretend they are delivering the cracker "letters" to mailboxes as they drop them one at a time into their mouth.

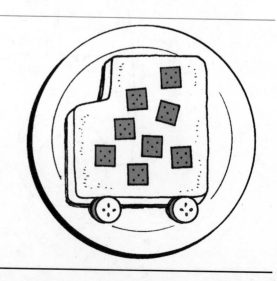

Take a Taxi

To play a variation of Follow the Leader, teach your children the following rhyme. Let one child at a time be the taxi driver who leads the way around the room. Have the other children follow behind. The driver holds onto a paper-plate "steering wheel" and makes the taxi go uphill and downhill by first walking high on tiptoe and then bending his or her knees to walk along as low as possible. Have the other children follow behind, copying the driver's up and down movements. Let the children take turns as the taxi driver, making the ride as hilly as they like!

Taxi driver, we need a ride.

That's my job – just hop inside.

I will take you all over town.

Some streets go up and some go down.

Durby Peterson

Pretend Armored Car

Let your children set up shop as storekeepers in various locations around the room. Give each one a supply of pretend dollar bills. (Out-dated store coupons work fine.) Explain that storekeepers sometimes call for an armored car to pick up their money and drive it to the bank. An armored car has extra-strong steel sides and is driven by guards who are specially trained to deliver the money safely. Place a metal toolbox on a small wagon to create a pretend armored car. Let your children take turns being the guard who drives the armored car around to collect money from the storekeepers and take it to the bank.

Parking Meter Play

Parking enforcement officers drive small, three-wheeled vehicles that resemble covered tricycles. They zip around town checking parking meters to make sure that people pay for the time they use a parking space.

Try this game the next time your group plays with riding toys. Trace from 1 to 6 coins on plain white self-adhesive labels and attach them to six potato-crisp tubes. Tell your children that the tubes are parking meters. Give each of your children several small blocks. When they want to park their riding toys, they must count the number of coins on the meter and place that many blocks inside. Have one child pretend to be the parking officer. Help the officer collect and count the blocks. Place self-stick note "tickets" on the cars if the amount of blocks and coins don't match.

Hint: Monitor the spaces so that no one riding toy remains parked for more than a few minutes.

Variation: Play this game inside with small toy cars.

Number Meter

Parking meters are timers. When drivers place coins in a parking meter, they are buying a number of minutes to park. Make a number meter by collecting two same-size paper plates. Cut a pie-shaped wedge out of the front of one plate. Around the front edge of the other plate, write the numerals 1 to 6. Nest the cut plate on top of the numbered one. Then poke a hole through the centers of both plates and insert a brass paper fastener.

Invite your children to pretend they have just parked a car. What number of minutes do they want to park? Have each child pick a number from 1 to 6. Then invite that child to set the dial on the Math Meter so it displays that number.

Extension: If you wish, bring in a real timer for your children to explore.

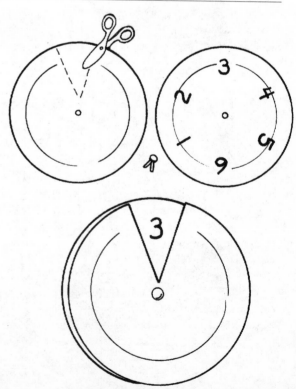

Sweep a Street

Turn a small toy vehicle into a street sweeper by taping an old paintbrush to the back of it so the bristles drag along the floor. Have your children use their street sweeper to sweep up sand in the sand table or sandbox.

Variation: Give each child a piece of paper. Instruct the children to tear the paper into a large dress box. As the children drive their cars inside the box, the brush will sweep up the paper.

Garbage Truck Song

Sung to: "Eensy Weensy Spider"

We pick up all the garbage

That's getting in the way.

In our big truck we carry it away.

That's how we keep the town so clean and bright.

We pick up all the garbage

And take it out of sight.

Durby Peterson

Gimme Garbage

Select a sturdy cardboard box with the top cut off. Help your children turn it into a "garbage truck" by gluing four black construction paper wheels onto the box sides. Add a rope to the front for pulling. After snacktime, let your children take turns pulling the garbage truck around. Have each child dump their garbage into the box. Teach them to sing "Garbage Truck Song" as they go.

Which Vehicle?

Select some large index cards. Make a simple drawing of a community service vehicle on each card. (See Page 49 for ideas, or simply photocopy and cut out the patterns, then glue them onto the cards.) Invite your children to sit in a circle, and fasten a card to the front of each child's shirt. Read the following statements and ask which vehicle is needed. As the group calls out the answer, let the child wearing the appropriate picture hop up and run around the circle. Continue until each child has had a turn.

The street is dirty with gravel and small bits of paper. Which vehicle does it need?

The mailbox is empty and waiting for some mail. Which vehicle does it need?

The garbage can is full and sitting by the road. Which vehicle does it need?

The parking meter is full of coins. Which vehicle does it need?

Vehicle Matchups

For each child, make a photocopy of page 49 and cut the pictures apart along the lines. (If your children are beginning to use scissors, let them help with the cutting.) Then mix up each child's set of pictures and place them on a table. Invite your children to match up each community service vehicle with the appropriate item that goes with it. Afterward, talk with them about the vehicles. Which ones have they seen around their town?

Matchup Patterns

Use with the activity on page 48.

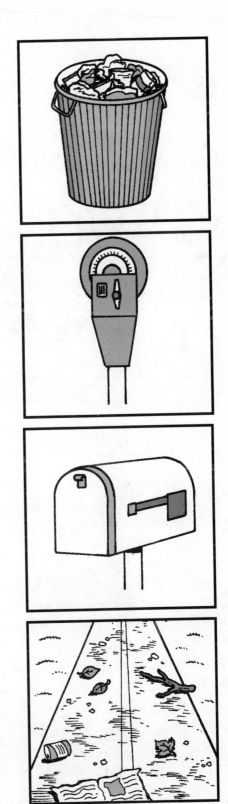

Construction Vehicles

Bulldozers

Bulldozers are large, strong vehicles meant to move dirt and clear the land for construction. They have a wide blade attached to the front that can knock down small trees and push dirt and rocks into huge piles.

Place a large toy bulldozer in your outdoor sandbox (or provide a few smaller bulldozers for the sand table). Encourage your children to take turns moving sand around to build imaginary structures and roads.

Hint: If you don't have any toy bulldozers, you can give your children 3-by-5-inch pieces of strong cardboard instead.

Bulldozer Art

Set out large pieces of fingerpainting paper and brown fingerpaint. Give each child a tongue depressor or a 3-by-5-inch piece of heavy cardboard. Drop a bit of paint on the paper in front of each child and let him or her use the tongue depressor or cardboard to push the paint around like bulldozers moving dirt.

Dump Trucks

Show your children toy dump trucks and pictures of real dump trucks. Discuss how dump trucks would be used on a construction site. They might be filled with leaves and small trees that need to be cleared, or dirt and rocks, or the remnants of a demolished building. What would your children dump if they had access to a dump truck?

Dump Truck Ditty

Sung to: "Frère Jacques"

When you're building, when you're clearing,

I'm right there, on alert.

I can carry rocks and other heavy stuff.

I can dump out the dirt.

Jaqueline Schiff

Dump Duty

Fill a large box or sensory tub with fresh potting soil. Let the children use spoons, small shovels, or toy cranes to load toy dump trucks with soil. When they have a full load, have the children drive the trucks to the potted plants in your facility and refresh the pots with the new soil.

Hint: Supervise carefully so the children don't sample your plants. Spread newspaper or a ground cloth underneath the box or tub to minimize mess.

Snack Truck

Serve your children individually wrapped snacks in a large toy dump truck. (Be sure to clean any dirt or sand from the truck ahead of time.) After each child selects a snack from the truck, have him or her "drive" the truck to the next child.

Concrete Mixer

Concrete mixing trucks are fascinating to young children. Explain how the back of the truck is like a giant mixing bowl and the chute is like a slide. Show pictures of a real cement mixer and discuss things that are made out of cement, such as some roads, certain parking garages, sidewalks, and parts of houses.

Mixer Song

Sung to: "Yankee Doodle"

I help build sidewalks, homes, and roads,

They say I am a fixer.

I have a drum that stirs wet paste,

I am a cement mixer.

Jacqueline Schiff

Mixing Fun

Set up a cooking or modeling dough activity that requires mixing. Let your children help you mix with large spoons. Later, explain that cement needs to be mixed just like their cooking project needed to be mixed. Since there is such a large amount of mixing to do, people who make cement find it easier to pour the ingredients into a cement mixer truck so the cement can be turned around and around to be mixed.

Making Cement

Let your children experiment by placing sand, water, and flour into a cylindrical container with a lid. Have them roll the can around to mix the ingredients together. Let them pour their "cement" into a plastic lid and let it set overnight.

Variation: This activity can be done with real cement, but be aware that it sets very quickly. It also is best to avoid handling wet cement (wear rubber gloves), as it is extremely drying to the skin.

CRANE

Cranes

When we drive by large construction sites, we usually see tall cranes. When constructing tall buildings, workers often need a quick, easy way to get heavy materials up to the top of their building. Many cranes look similar to bulldozers, but instead of having a shovel blade in front, they have a large, tall tower with a pulley attached. Workers secure building materials to one end of the pulley. The other end of the pulley is weighted so that it will move slowly downward while the materials move slowly upward. When the materials reach the desired height, workers waiting there take them off. If possible, bring in pictures of cranes and a toy crane. Let your children play with the toy crane in the block area.

Cranes, Cranes

Cranes, cranes, everywhere,

Building skyscrapers in the air.

Wood and steel (text garbled here), up they go—

Lots of buildings in a row.

Jean Warren

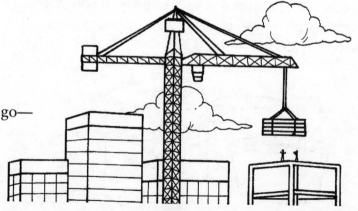

Construction Problem Solving

This activity will really get your children into problem solving. Order a load of new sand for your outdoor sandbox, or a load of dirt for your gardening area. Let your children enjoy watching as the dump truck comes and delivers the load. Ahead of time, arrange for the load to be dumped a short distance away from your sandbox or gardening area. After the truck leaves, ask the children how they think they can get the load where it belongs. Encourage your children to devise ways to carry the dirt or sand.

Some may fill buckets and carry the dirt or sand. Others may fill up a wagon and pull it over to the site. This project could last for up to a month, but the learning that takes place is well worth the time. When the sand or dirt is in the right place, ask your children to help you organize a celebration for a job well done.

Construction Site Project

You may find that your study of construction vehicles leads naturally into a construction site project. The following activities are ideas to get your children started.

Setting Up Your Site

Use plastic tape to mark off a large area in your play yard. Ask your children what they would like to build at their construction site. You might give them some options, such as a small house, a yard or garden, a dog-house, or a patio or deck. After your children decide what they want to construct and what materials they will need to construct it, arrange to have the materials delivered to your site.

For example, if your children wanted to build a patio, help them mark off a square with chalk. Ask parents to assist the children in framing the square, and then have a cement patio poured into the frame. Your children will really get a good idea of a construction site, and they will have a new area in their play yard.

Field Trip

If possible, take a field trip to a local construction site. (The city planner's office should be able to give you the names and phone numbers of the contractors in charge of nearby sites.) Ask the contractor or site manager to tell your children what is being built, and what stage has been reached in the building process. Invite him or her to show your group any construction vehicles at the site and to explain how they are being used. Be sure to set aside some time for the children to ask questions.

Variation: If a field trip is not realistic, make arrangements with a contractor to bring a construction vehicle to your school. You could also arrange for a construction worker to visit your class. Ask him or her to bring some special handheld equipment or clothing worn on a construction site.

Dressing for Safety

The following clothing and equipment suggestions are used at construction sites for safety while building. Ask a construction worker to come in and show the children each of the mentioned items and explain why it is needed at a construction site. Have child-size items available for whoever is working in your classroom construction site. Be sure to outfit yourself, too.

Hard Hats—Have your children paint the outsides of large paper bowls with orange paint. When they are dry, let the children wear them as pretend hard hats.

Safety Vests—Have each child paint the outside of a large grocery sack with bright yellow paint. Starting from the bottom of the sack cut a seam down the middle of one of the long sides until you reach the sack's bottom. Then cut a big neck hole in the bottom of the sack. Cut armholes on both of the sack's short sides. Let the children stick their arms through the armholes. (You may need to trim the bottom of the sack for very small children.)

Construction Cones—Show your children how to roll large sheets of orange construction paper into cone shapes. Tape the cones at the seam to secure. You may need to trim them at the bottom so that they stand upright. Have the children use the cones to mark off their pretend construction sites.

Tool Belts—Bring in fanny packs or real tool belts to hold the children's small construction tools.

Work Gloves—Ask parents to help you collect work or garden gloves for your children to wear in their Construction Zone.

Safety Goggles—Safety goggles can be purchased inexpensively at most hardware stores. Or invite the children to bring in sunglasses or water goggles for make believe eye protection.

Delivery Vehicles

Delivery Trucks

Discuss delivery trucks with your children. Can they name a type of delivery truck (mail truck, milk delivery truck, diaper delivery truck, etc.)?

Encourage your children to pretend to be delivery vehicles during dramatic playtime. In your dress-up area, provide props such as empty pizza boxes, a tote bag with envelopes inside, grocery bags, fake flowers, and empty milk cartons.

Delivery Truck Drivers

Arrange for drivers of a variety of delivery trucks to speak to your children about their work. If they make regular deliveries, have them talk about the routes they take, and what they do to prepare for deliveries each day. Encourage them to bring in examples of the type of paperwork they use. Before the visit, have the children think of questions to ask, such as "How do you load and unload the deliveries? Do you drive by yourself or do you have a partner? What happens when no one is home to receive a delivery? Have you ever gotten lost?" If possible, try to obtain permission to allow the children to climb inside each truck.

Package Delivery

Order a surprise for your children and have it delivered to your room. Arrange for the delivery person to come to your room and spend a short time answering questions about his or her job and giving the children a tour of the delivery truck.

Loading Helpers

Loading and unloading boxes is hard work. Often delivery drivers use a cart called a dolly or hand truck to stack their packages on and to roll them into the area where they need to be delivered. If possible, bring in a dolly and some boxes with a little weight in them. Help one child at a time move one or two boxes around the room. Can the children think of anything else in the room that needs to be moved with the dolly?

Truck Art

Attach large delivery truck shapes to your easels. Let your children paint the trucks to represent delivery trucks they have seen. Then attach the trucks to the wall at the children's eye level to create a delivery truck border or mural.

Food Delivery Riddles

Tell your children the following riddles. At the end of each riddle, ask the children to name the food delivery truck it describes. Have any of them had food or other items delivered to their homes?

I ring my chimes

And the children scream,

For I'm filled with sweet treats—

Cold and yummy ice cream!

Which truck am I?

You order the toppings,

You order the size,

I come to your door

With fresh-baked pizza pies.

Which truck am I?

I work for a dairy

Where cows freely roam.

Their milk goes into cartons

I bring to your home.

Which truck am I?

Jacqueline Schiff

Ice Cream Trucks

Have your children ever seen an ice cream delivery truck? Have they ever purchased ice cream from an ice cream truck? How do they know when an ice cream truck is near? If possible, bring in a recording of an instrumental version of "Pop! Goes the Weasel" (this is the song many ice cream trucks play). Ask parents to send in ice cream bar boxes they may have. Let your children play the recording and dramatize being ice cream delivery truck drivers.

Hint: You can make ice cream bars for your children to "sell" by attaching ice cream bar shapes to craft sticks.

The Ice Cream Truck

Sung to: "Row, Row, Row Your Boat"

Ring, ring, down the street

Comes the ice cream truck.

It will have my favorite kind

If I have any luck.

Jean Warren

I Love Chocolate

Sung to: "Frère Jacques"

I love chocolate,

I love chocolate

Ice cream,

Ice cream.

Yummy, yummy ice cream,

Yummy, yummy ice cream.

Yes indeed,

Yes indeed.

Jean Warren

Pizza Truck Dramatics

Children love to pretend to deliver pizzas. If possible, show your children pictures of pizza delivery vehicles (check the Sunday newspaper for advertisements). Explain to your children that some pizza companies have delivery trucks while other companies let pizza delivery people use their own vehicles. Have your children noticed whether pizza delivered to their homes came in trucks or other vehicles?

Extension: If possible, order a pizza to be delivered to your room. Arrange for the delivery person to spend some time answering questions your children may have, and showing them his or her vehicle and the container used to keep the pizzas warm.

Pizza Delivery Sign

Set out several 5-by-10-inch pieces of heavy cardboard. Ask your children to brainstorm pizza parlor names. Write the names on the pieces of cardboard and have your children decorate them. Let the children attach the signs to trikes and wagons and then pretend to deliver pizzas to each other.

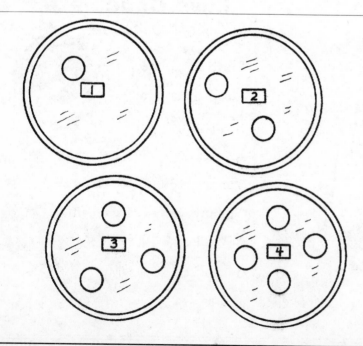

Pepperoni Pizza Game

In a work center, set out four pizza pans. Use masking tape to number the pans from 1 to 4. Cut ten pepperoni-size circles out of red felt. Let your children take turns placing the appropriate number of pepperoni slices in each pan.

Variation: If you don't have pizza pans available, cut large circles out of gray felt.

Food Delivery Trucks

Many trucks deliver foods to stores, restaurants, and people's homes. Ask the children if they have ever seen a milk delivery truck if they have had milk delivered to their home. If possible, find a few milk crates (try asking a dairy for old ones). Rinse out several small half-gallon milk cartons. Keep the cartons and milk crates in your dramatic play area and let your children deliver milk to each other.

Delivering Snacks

Place each child's snack in a plastic bag and place the bags in a wagon. Fill another wagon with juice boxes or small cartons of milk. At snacktime, let your children take turns delivering the food to the other children seated at the table.

Truck Driver Song

Sung to: "Do Your Ears Hang Low?"

Well, I drive a truck

And I carry lots of stuff.

I bring food to stores,

Then I go deliver more.

If you wave to me

I will honk back merrily,

'Cause I love driving trucks.

Diane Thom

Emergency Vehicles

Emergency Matchup

Ambulances, fire trucks, and police cars are the most common emergency vehicles. Provide your children with pictures or models of these vehicles, or copy the vehicle patterns on page 69. The pattern cards on pages 70 and 71 include items that are associated with each vehicle. Talk about what these items are used for, and have the children sort and match them to the correct emergency vehicle.

Hint: Your local fire and police departments are great resources for safety materials.

Vehicle Dispatch

Cut out the emergency vehicle patterns on page 69. Back them with flannel, and arrange all three vehicles on your flannelboard. Then have the children pretend that they are 9-1-1 dispatchers. Give each child small flannel scraps to use as markers. As you talk about emergency situations, encourage the children to place markers by the vehicles they would send to help out. (During a fire, you would send a fire truck. If someone were lost, you would send a police car.) Have the children explain their choices. Explain that in some emergencies, more than one type of vehicle could be appropriate. Accept all logical answers. Let the children count the markers to see which emergency vehicle they would use the most.

Extension: Talk with your children about when it's appropriate to call 9-1-1. Should you call if you are lost? If you see an accident or fire? What if your cat is stuck in a tree? Explain that 9-1-1 is for people emergencies only, not for pets. Remind the children to stay on the phone line during a real emergency until the 9-1-1 operator gives instructions to hang up.

Our Fire Truck

Bring in a large cardboard box. Have your children work together to use the box to build a fire truck. Collect picture books about fire trucks or plan a visit to your local fire station so they can view a fire truck firsthand. Encourage the children to come up with their own ideas for finding or making props that will enhance their play. For example, a piece of PVC tubing could become a fire hose. Square holes cut into a rectangular piece of cardboard makes an effective pretend ladder. Facilitate your group's pretend play as long as interest lasts.

Extension: If you wish, build police cars and ambulances. Extend your children's emergency vehicle play into a larger group project by creating a fire station, police station, or hospital in your room. Invite emergency personnel such as firefighters, police officers, or paramedics to visit and talk about what they do and what it's like to work in these settings.

Rescue Teams

Firefighters, police officers, and paramedics travel to emergencies in teams of two or more people. Working in teams makes it easier and safer for these community helpers to do their jobs. Throughout the day, encourage your children to play and work together in pairs or small groups. If you wish, assign each "team" a mini-"rescue" project around your room, such as watering the plants, straightening the play area, or washing and fixing toys.

Firefighter Hats

For each child, use red construction paper (or newspaper painted red) to make a folded paper firefighter hat. (See the illustration below.) Secure all loose edges with tape. Fold up one corner of each hat and staple it in place. Then attach a yellow construction paper badge shape.

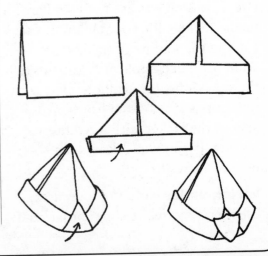

Ambulance Game

Ambulances and other emergency vehicles travel very quickly when they are needed to rush ill or injured people to the hospital. Their sirens and flashing lights warn people that they are coming. At the sound of sirens, drivers move their cars, trucks, and other vehicles to the side of the road to let ambulances get through.

Explain to your children that if they hear a siren, they should stop what they are doing and find an adult. Play the following game to help them practice stopping when they hear a siren or an alarm. Let two children pretend to be ambulances while the rest pretend to be cars and trucks driving down the road. Give the "ambulances" a bell and a flashlight. When the ambulances ring their bell or turn on their flashlights, the cars and trucks need to stop moving and move out of the way. Let any child who wishes to have a turn as an ambulance.

Variation: Place this game outside using riding toys. Have your children pretend to be other emergency vehicles, such as police cars and fire trucks.

Paramedic Jacket

Use an old pillowcase to make Paramedic Jackets for your children. Cut a slit in the middle of the bottom seam for a neck hole and two slits in the side seams for armholes. Draw a red cross shape on the front or the arm of the jacket with a red fabric marker. If you wish, draw on a pocket, as well.

Variation: Instead of pillow cases, use men's old white shirts or jackets.

Emergency Kit

Find an old lunch box or tackle box, and have your children attach a red cross shape to the top using red tape. Explain to the children that the red cross is a safety symbol. Fill the box with first-aid supplies for a group pretend play emergency kit. Keep the box in your dress-up area. Consider including the following safety items:

- Adhesive bandages
- Gauze bandages
- Cotton balls
- Splinter tweezers
- Antiseptic wipes
- Artificial ice pack
- Safety light (or a flashlight with working batteries)
- Safety blanket

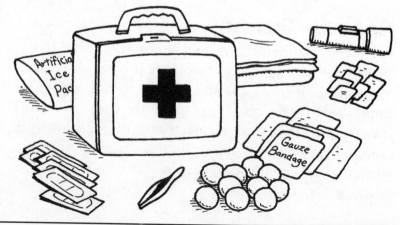

Police Car Song

Sung to: "She'll Be Coming Round the Mountain"

A police car with flashing lights on top

Keeps the city safe and makes the traffic stop.

Look what wears a badge so proudly,

And whose siren blows so loudly:

A police car with flashing lights on top.

Diane Thom

Police Badges

For each of your children, cut a star shape out of large plain white stickers, such as those sold at office supply stores for address labels. Provide the children with gray or silver crayons or markers and let them decorate their stickers. Or set out small aluminum foil pieces for them to glue onto their shapes. Use a black marker to write "Police" on the middle of each sticker badge.

Hint: Keep a name card nearby with the word "Police" written on it for older preschoolers to trace and copy.

Traffic Jam

Put masking tape on the floor to represent a four-way intersection, as shown in the illustration. Have your children pretend to drive cars and trucks that are approaching the intersection from different directions. You play the police officer directing traffic. Stand in the intersection (with a whistle to blow, if possible). Invite your children to grip their "steering wheels," and make their engines "vroom" and their horns honk. Blow the whistle and motion one line of children across the intersection at a time. Let the children who cross the intersection get in the back of another line and approach it from a different direction

Extension: Add to the excitement by pretending to notice one vehicle speeding. Jump into your imaginary police car, turn on your siren, and race after the speeding motorist. Give the motorist a friendly warning about driving safely, and then return to the intersection to continue directing traffic.

Sirens

Most emergency vehicles have sirens and flashing lights mounted on top of them. The sound of sirens can be frightening for preschoolers. Explain to your children that sirens are really helpers because they let people know that there is an emergency. If you wish, tape the sound of a real siren for your children to listen to. Talk about other sounds that warn of danger or an emergency, such as fire alarms, car horns, train whistles, and severe-weather warning bells. Invite the children to discuss any loud sounds that frighten them.

Siren Song

Sung to: "Twinkle, Twinkle, Little Star"

When you hear a siren's sound—

Ding! Ding! Ding! Ding!—please slow down.

Help is coming very fast.

Stop and let the ambulance pass.

When you hear a siren's sound,

Help is coming; please slow down.

Substitute the names of other emergency vehicles, such as *fire truck* and *police car*, for *ambulance*.

Carol Gnojewski

Emergency Snack

During emergencies, food and water can be hard to come by. That's why it's important to keep a supply of bottled water and high-energy, nonperishable food. Serve your children a snack of food you might keep for an emergency, such as granola bars, dried fruit, chocolate, or beef jerky. Provide bottled water for them to drink.

Emergency Vehicle Patterns

Use with the activity on page 64.

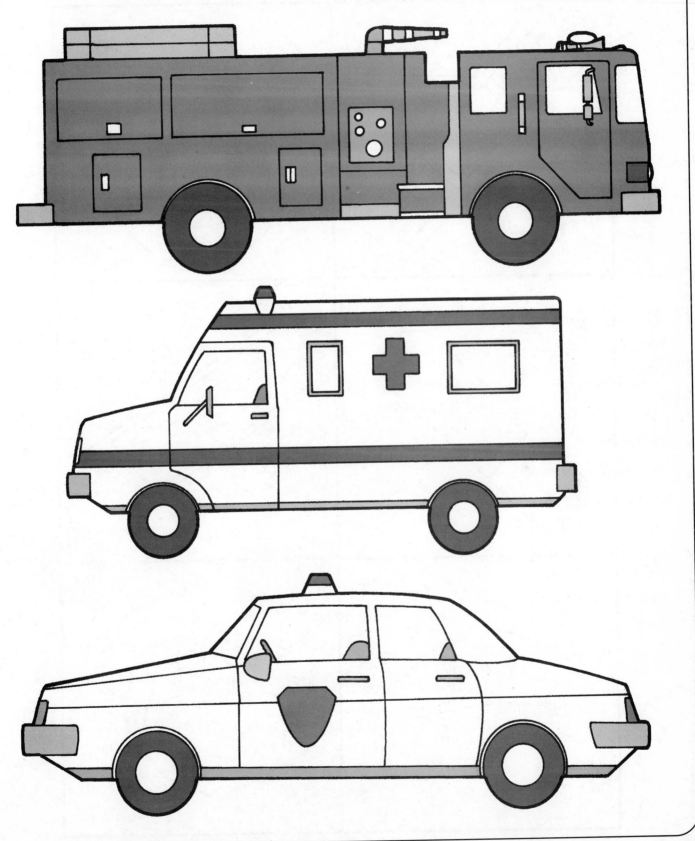

Pattern Cards

Use with the activity on page 64.

Pattern Cards

Use with the activity on page 64.

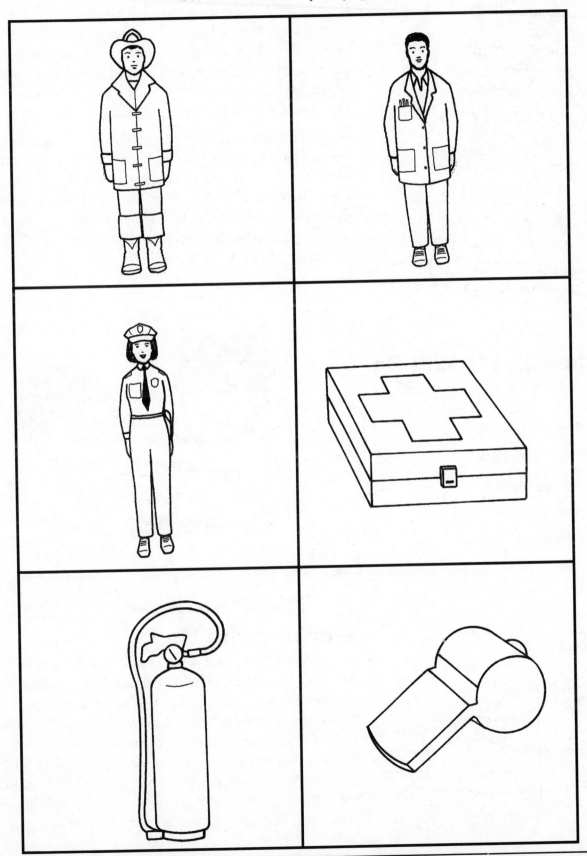

Farm Vehicles

Tractors

Because tractors can do so many things, they are one of the most important vehicles on a farm. Before tractors were invented, jobs like plowing (loosening the dirt so it is easier to plant seeds) were done by hand or by horse-drawn plows. Now, depending on how big their fields are, farmers can use tractors to plow their fields in a matter of hours instead of days.

Give each of your children a small shovel and take them outdoors. Find a patch of dirt that is hard (or firmly pack down an area of dirt). Ask your children to "plow" by turning over shovelsful of dirt. Later, discuss how hard it would be to use shovels to plow a field of dirt as large as your play yard (or some other relevant space of land). Wouldn't it be nice to have a tractor to do the work for them?

A-Plowing We Will Go

Sung to: "The Farmer in the Dell"

A-plowing we will go,

A-plowing we will go,

Let's plow the field

To plant some corn.

Then we'll watch it grow.

Substitute the names of other farm crops in place of *corn*.

Carol Gnojewski

Working the Soil

Use a shovel to remove a big chunk of dirt from your play yard. Set the dirt in a bucket or plastic tub. Invite your children to help you explore the dirt clod by using fingers, sticks, small shovels, or toy farm vehicles to drill holes, make furrows, and break up the soil into small pieces. Explain that these are some of the activities that farm machinery are used for. When you are finished exploring, enlist the help of your children to refill the hole in your play yard, and rake the soil smooth around it.

Fast and Slow

Tractors usually move very slowly. If you happen to see a tractor on a country road, you may wish it would move faster. But faster is not always better. For plowing, mowing, and other tasks tractors perform, slower is better.

Practice fast and slow concepts with this game. Have your children form a circle. When you call out the name of a vehicle, have your children move faster or slower, as that vehicle would move. For example, call out the names of the following vehicles: racecar, truck, bicycle, train, and tractor.

Observing Tractors

* Add books about tractors to your reading area.
* Place toy tractors in your block area or sand table.
* Display pictures of tractors around your room.
* Explore a real tractor at a farm or a farm equipment store.

Out in the Field

Sung to: "Down by the Station"

Out in the field

Early in the morning,

See the red tractor

Digging in the dirt.

See the busy farmer

Riding on the tractor;

Plow, plow, plow, plow

Up the dirt.

As you sing this song, have your children pretend to be tractors plowing dirt.

Jean Warren

Wagons

Wagons are very useful vehicles on a farm. Sometimes they are small wagons that are pulled by hand and used to gather vegetables and flowers as they are picked. Sometimes they are large wagons pulled by horses or tractors. Farmers use large wagons out in the fields. As they harvest their crops, farmers place them in baskets or crates and stack them on a wagon. Have your children pretend to harvest vegetables and place them in a wagon as they sing the following song.

Sung to: "The Paw-Paw Patch"

Harvesting the crops and putting 'em in the wagon,

Harvesting the crops and putting 'em in the wagon,

Harvesting the crops and putting 'em in the wagon,

Way down yonder in the vegetable patch.

Jean Warren

Crop Count

Talk about the different crops that farmers plant with the help of tractors and other farm machinery. If you wish, bring in seed catalogs that show pictures of farm crops. Make a list of all of the crops that your children name and draw a small picture by each one.

Then have your children line up in three or four rows. Make sure they are all facing forward. Help them spread out a bit so that they each have some "elbow room." Invite the children to pretend that you are a farmer and they are all new plants growing in your field. Give each child a few minutes to think about what type of crop from your list he or she would like to be. When they are ready, have the children crouch down very low to the floor. Call out the name of a specific crop, such as tomatoes. All the "tomatoes" should then "grow" (stand up) and count off. Continue with other crop names, until all crops have been accounted for.

Variation: Select a child to be the farmer and call out the name of a crop. After the crop "grows," the child should then count the number of plants. The farmer then selects one of the plants he has counted to take his place.

Hay Wagons

When harvesting hay, farmers first cut the hay, then bale (bundle) the hay, and then they use wagons to transport the bales from the field to the barn. Provide your children with a pile of hay (available at feed stores) and encourage them to load the hay into a small wagon, pull it across the play yard, and unload it. Let everyone have a turn loading and transporting the hay. (Be aware of any known hay or alfalfa allergies before bringing hay into the room.)

Hayrides

In the fall, after the hay was cut and stored, farmers would often celebrate by having a hayride. They filled their wagons with hay and took their friends and family for a ride. Everyone sat in the back of the wagon on the hay and visited and sang songs. Let your children take turns getting into a wagon filled with hay while you pull them around the play yard.

Hayride Song

Sung to: "Up on the Housetop"

Hey! Hey! Hey! Let's take a ride
Over the fields and countryside.
Hitch up a wagon filled with hay,
Climb aboard to sing and play.

Hey! Hey! Hey! Hey! Hey! Hey!
Let's take a long hayride today.
We'll hitch up the tractor to a wagon of hay,
And climb aboard to sing and play.

Carol Gnojewski

Wheelbarrows

Wheelbarrows are one-wheeled wagons that farmers use to move things from one place to another. Wheelbarrows differ from wagons in two main ways—they only have one wheel, and they are pushed instead of pulled. Bring in a small wheelbarrow for your children to experience. Encourage them to experiment by transporting items first with a wagon and then with a wheelbarrow. Which mode of transport to they prefer?

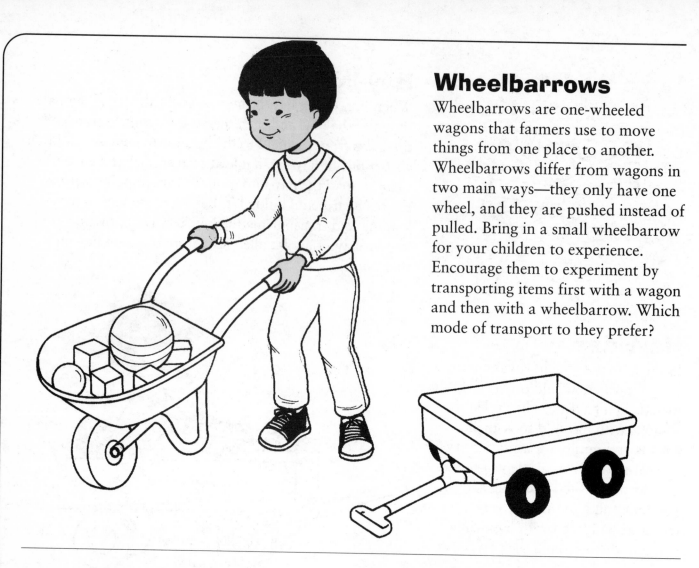

Counting Wheels

Give each of your children four circle shapes cut from cardboard. Call out the name of a vehicle and have the children set out the correct number of wheels the vehicle has. Try calling out the following vehicle names: car, bike, wagon, wheelbarrow, truck, trike, and so on.

Bike

Farm Vehicles

Farms are filled with a variety of vehicles. If your children show more interest in farm vehicles, you may want to explore some of the following ideas.

- Call the John Deere corporation and ask for several catalogs. Your children will enjoy looking through the catalogs and guessing the purpose of each piece of equipment.

- Explore your local library for books about farms and farm equipment. You may also come across videos that show farm equipment in use.

- Talk about how trucks are used in farming. Ask a farmer to come in and talk about trucks and other farm vehicles.

Gas Stations

Our Gas Station

Invite your children to help you set up a gas station in the home-life area. Help them think about what a gas station is like by reading them related books or providing them with pictures. Talk about some of your own experiences in gas stations, and encourage the children to relate any experiences they may have had.

Then help the children make a list of the products and equipment they want their gas station to have. Guide their thinking by asking them questions. Is it a self-serve station (where customers pump gas for themselves) or a full-service station (where employees called gas or service attendants pump gas for customers)? Does it have a garage for car repair work? Will it include a convenience store for small items such as soda, oil, milk, maps, and candy? How many gas pumps will it have? What about a car wash?

Encourage them to come up with questions of their own. Together, think of ways to find out the answers. Perhaps you will need to invite a gas station employee to talk to the children, or take a field trip to a local gas station. Help the children come up with ideas for making or collecting the items that they will need to make their station complete.

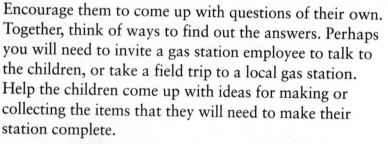

Drive-Through Car Wash

Lay a large cardboard appliance box on its side and cut off both ends. Reinforce the box by wrapping tape around its sides. On the inside of the box, hang a row of fabric strips from the "ceiling" across the midpoint. Then have your children ride their tricycles and other riding toys through the "car wash."

Gas Pump

Cut a small hole in the side of a medium-sized cardboard box. Cut off three or four feet from the end of an old garden hose. Insert the cut end of the hose into the hole in the box and securely tape it in place. Attach a pistol-grip nozzle to the other end of the hose. Add "gas pump" details to the box with felt-tip markers, as desired. Talk about why it's important to fill cars with gas (to keep them running).

Car Mechanic

Invite a real mechanic into your classroom to talk about what they do (fix cars) and where they work (gas station, car repair shop, or car garage). Have him or her bring in some of the tools car mechanics need, and maybe some car parts. Encourage the mechanic to use and explain new words such as *jack*, *car hood*, and *engine*.

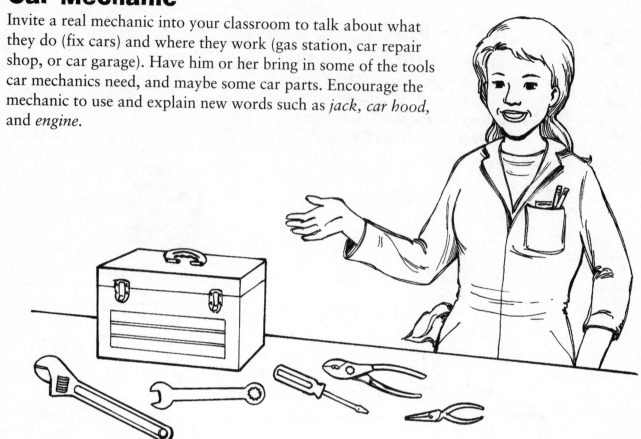

Air Pump

Bring in a bicycle pump, a tire pressure gauge, and a spare tire. Show your children how to find the air pressure in the tire using the pressure gauge. Then attach the pump to the tire and help the children pump more air into the tire. Check the pressure of the tire again. Is the number on the gauge higher or lower now? Invite the children to explain why.

Hint: Younger preschoolers will enjoy simply experimenting with the air pump.

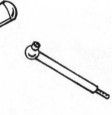

Fuel Snack

To keep your children's "motors" running, let them fuel up with a snack of boxed fruit juice and round crackers. Let the children pretend that the juice boxes are gas pumps as they sip through the straws to fill up their "tanks." Have the children count out four round cracker "tires" to eat as well.

Make It Shine

Bring in a variety of car cleaning supplies such as soapy water, sponges, and chamois cloths. Explain to your children that, along with keeping a car fueled with gas and oil, keeping it clean on the inside and out helps a car stay in good shape. Then set out toy cars, trucks, and other vehicles, along with accessories such as ramps, garages, and toy ladders. Provide your children with small cups of water, small paint brushes, and paper towels. Let the children use the water and brushes to wash the cars. Have them use the paper towels (and the chamois cloth, if you wish) to polish them dry.

Mini Tow Trucks

Attach self-stick velcro strips to the front and back ends of small toy trucks and cars. Your children will have fun sticking the velcro strips together to tow cars around your room.

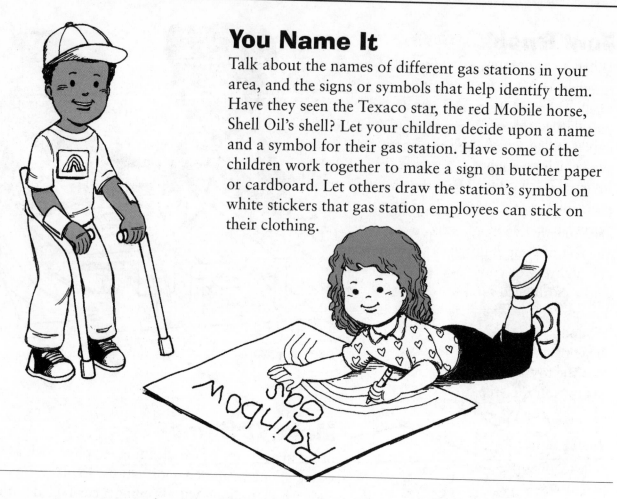

You Name It

Talk about the names of different gas stations in your area, and the signs or symbols that help identify them. Have they seen the Texaco star, the red Mobile horse, Shell Oil's shell? Let your children decide upon a name and a symbol for their gas station. Have some of the children work together to make a sign on butcher paper or cardboard. Let others draw the station's symbol on white stickers that gas station employees can stick on their clothing.

Trip to the Gas Station

Sung to: "I Know an Old Lady"

Let's stop at the station

To fill up the tank.

The gas light says *E*,

Which means it's empty.

We'll give our car gas, then check the oil;

The car will spoil if it doesn't have oil.

We'll add some oil and check for air;

Your tires can get flat if you don't do that.

Then we'll wash the windows before we go

And after all that, we might need a map

To find our way back.

Carol Gnojewski

Tow Truck Game

When a car or truck is no longer drivable, a tow truck is needed to pull or carry it to a gas station or car repair shop. The two most common tow trucks are hook trucks and flatbed trucks. Hook trucks use a pulley crane and cables called *winches* to strap the front or back tires of the vehicle to a wheel lift. Flatbeds have ramps that are lowered so that the vehicle can be pulled up onto its flat truck bed.

Pick one or two children to be tow truck operators while the rest of your children pretend to be cars driving down the highway of your room or play yard. Provide a wagon and a cardboard ramp to use as a flatbed tow truck. Encourage the "cars" to splutter and fall down to the ground as they run out of gas or pop their tires. Help the "tow truck" operators use the ramp to move the "cars" into the tow truck. Tow the "broken" cars to your group gas station for "repairs"

Let each child have a turn as a tow truck operator.

Variation: Have the children drive toy cars around your room. Substitute the wagon for a working pulley or toy tow truck.

Jack It Up

Bring in an automotive jack for your children to experiment with. Explain that a jack is a lever used by tow truck operators and mechanics to raise one side of a car or truck off the ground. Place the jack under one side of a wagon or large riding toy. Show your children how to pump the jack handle up and down in order to lift the jack. Invite the children to spin the raised wheels. Why might it be important to raise a car with a jack to change a flat tire? If you wish, let your children observe mechanics as they use a jack or a hydraulic lift to service a vehicle at your local gas station or car repair shop.

Hint: Supervise carefully, especially during raising or lifting, to avoid pinched fingers and toes.

Extension: Explore other levers with your children, including shovels, crowbars, light switches, and seesaws.

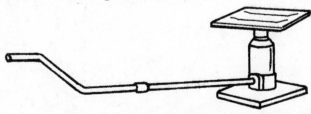

Horse-Drawn Vehicles

A Horse of a Different Color

Horses pull all types of horse-drawn vehicles, which come in many different shapes and sizes. They were also used for different types of work, such as racing, delivering mail and other goods, and carrying passengers. Show your children pictures of different types of horse-drawn vehicles, including the Horse-Drawn Vehicle illustrations on pages 88–89. (If you wish, back these illustrations with felt and arrange them on your flannelboard.) Have your children compare these vehicles. How many wheels do they have? How many horses are pulling them? Which would be best for carrying heavy things? Which would be best for racing? Which would they like to drive or ride in?

Variation: Have the children compare the horse-drawn vehicles to cars, trains, airplanes, and tractors, which replaced many of these vehicles as faster modes of transportation. Explain that cars were first called horseless carriages.

Giddyup! Whoa!

Invite your children to pretend to be a team of horses while you are the wagon or carriage driver. Help the children line up in two rows facing forward. Stand in back of the two rows. Explain that when you yell "Giddyup!" the "horses" should then begin to walk forward. When you yell "Whoa!" they should stop. Lead your team around your room or along an indoor or outdoor trail that you have marked off with chalk or tape. Instruct them to go faster or slower as you see fit. Periodically, have them stop and start again. If you wish, let each child who wants to have a turn as the driver.

Extension: Provide "horse snacks" (apple slices and carrot sticks) at the end of the trail.

Kid Power

Horsepower is the rate of work of one horse. It is a way of measuring power. For example, a car might have a 280-horsepower engine. Try the following experiment to measure the "kid power" of your children.

Mark off a short distance (two or three yards) by drawing a line with chalk or tape. Place an empty wagon at the beginning of the line. Have your children completely fill the wagon with a load of books. Then see how many of them it takes to pull and push the loaded wagon to the end of the line. Try the same experiment using other materials in your room, such as blocks, stuffed animals, or dress-up clothes. Make a Kid Power Chart to record your findings. Afterward, congratulate the children for how strong they are!

Shoe Print Horse Head

Give each of your children a piece of construction paper. Have the children put one foot in the middle of the paper. Use a marker to trace the outline of each child's shoe on the paper. Help the children cut triangles for ear shapes and glue them on top of the print as shown in the illustration. Provide pictures of horses for your children to look at. Then set out crayons or markers and let them draw in eyes and decorate their horses as they see fit.

Giddyup, Horsey
Sung to: "Camptown Races"

Giddyup, horsey,

Let's go to town,

To town,

To town.

Giddyup, horsey,

Let's go to town

In our buckboard.

Additional verses: In our covered wagon; In our carriage; in our stagecoach.

Jean Warren

Covered Wagon Train

Explain to your children that pioneers moving west traveled together in wagon trains. Each family's covered wagon was like a separate car in a choo-choo train.

Make a covered wagon (or wagons) by bending and taping a large piece of posterboard over the top of an ordinary wagon. Let the children fill the wagon with "supplies" for a pretend trip. Then arrange their wagons and riding vehicles in a line. Have the children travel across your room in their wagon train.

Wagon Circle

At night, members of wagon trains often arranged their wagons in a circle for protection. Inside the wagon circle, the pioneers felt safe. They would take time to play, eat, and sleep. Enlist your children's help in making a wagon circle using large blocks or pillows for wagons. Designate the Wagon Circle as a place for children to go when they want to rest or read quietly.

Hint: You may want to limit the amount of children who can gather in the Wagon Circle at one time.

Wagon Train Countdown Song

Sung to: "When Johnny Comes Marching Home"

We're riding in a wagon train. Giddyup! Giddyup!

We're riding in a wagon train. Giddyup! Giddyup!

We have six horses in our team

To carry us over the hills and streams.

Oh, we're bound for new land in our wagon train.

Repeat, decreasing the number of horses in the third line each time. Have the children hold up that many fingers.

Carol Gnojewski

Carriages

Before cars were invented, people traveled in carriages. Some carriages were plain and some were fancy.

Buckboards—These carriages were plain and were used to haul supplies from town to people's farms and homes.

Surreys—These carriages were fancy and were used to visit friends or go to church.

- Encourage your children to use their wagons as carriages. Let one child pretend to be the horse and pull the wagon.

- If your children want to make a surrey, give them materials to build a fringed sun roof for their wagon.

Coaches

Coaches were carriages that were totally enclosed. Stagecoaches were pulled by four or more horses. They were used to travel far distances from town to town. Stagecoaches were also used to carry mail and packages.

Provide your children with large cardboard boxes to use to create a stagecoach.

Fantasy Coaches

Many folk and fairy tales, such as Cinderella, Robin Hood, Pinocchio, and Paul Bunyan, include passages that describe rides in horse-drawn vehicles such as coaches, carriages, and carts. Consider adapting such a tale for your children. Let them help you describe what the coach, carriage, or cart would look like, and how it would feel to ride in it.

Hint: If you celebrate Christmas in your facility, a tale about Santa and his reindeer-pulled sleigh would also be appropriate.

Extension: As a follow-up activity, invite your children to draw or paint the coach in your story.

Horse-Drawn Vehicles

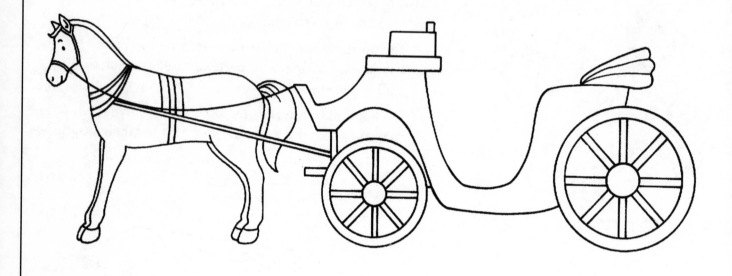

Motorcycles

Motorcycles

Motorcycles are like bikes with motors. Most children have seen motorcycles and are interested in them because of the noise they make, the gear the motorcyclists wear, and simply because they look like fun. Motorcycles can go almost anywhere. They can travel both on regular roads and long dirt paths. Discuss motorcycles with your children.

🏍 Where would they travel if they owned a motorcycle?

🏍 What would they call their motorcycle if they gave it a name?

🏍 What would they wear if they were riding a motorcycle? This is a good opportunity to introduce the importance of wearing helmets and other safety gear when riding on a motorcycle.

Motorcycle Movement

Invite your children to pretend that they are riding motorcycles. Have them stamp or kick their feet down to kick-start their engines. Then have them pretend to rev up their engines by turning the controls on their handlebars. Encourage them to make motorcycle noises as they race, zoom, and jump their bikes around your room.

Patrol Duty

Did your children know that community helpers such as police officers and forest rangers sometimes use motorcycles in their work? Invite a forest ranger or police officer from a motorcycle patrol to visit your group. If possible, have them bring along their motorcycle. Encourage them to show children the parts of their motorcycle, and to explain how the motorcycle helps them in their work.

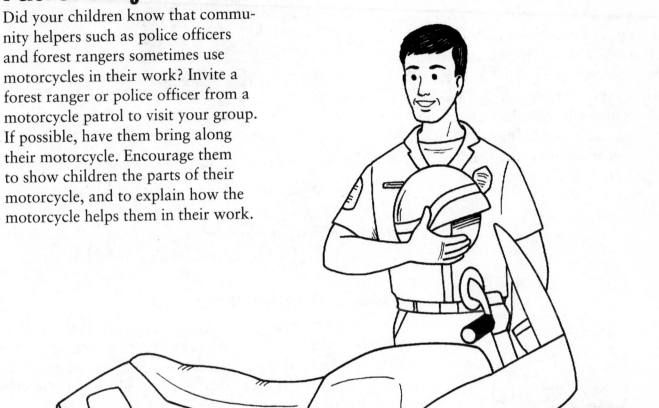

Wheelie Art

Find a small toy motorcycle with rubber wheels that turn. Let your children dip the wheels into shallow containers of paint and then drive the motorcycle back and forth on a large piece of newsprint.

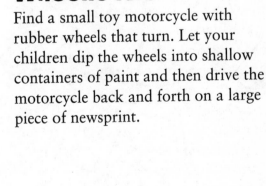

Weather Wear

When riding on a motorcycle, it is important to dress for the weather. Ask your children what they would wear if they were going for a motorcycle ride. Discuss the fact that when you ride on a motorcycle, it is very windy, and sometimes cold. Talk about how this is similar to the wind coming in through an open car window. Explain to your children that leather gear is popular for motorcyclists because it is warm and wind resistant.

Motorcycle Dress-up

Riding gear helps a motorcyclist stay comfortable in all kinds of weather conditions, and prevents or reduces injuries. Bring in the following motorcycle safety gear. Talk about where each piece is worn and what it is used for. If possible, keep the gear in your dress-up area for pretend motorcycle play.

- **Motorcycle Helmet**—Helps protect your head against injury, wind, cold, and flying objects.

- **Face shield**—Helps protect the face against rocks, insects, and other debris.

- **Leather Gloves**—Keep hands warm and protect them against scrapes.

- **Leather Jacket**—Resists wind and protects against cold and sunburn.

- **Long Pants**—Protects limbs against cold, sunburn, and scrapes.

- **Boots**—Protect your feet and provide good grip on pedals, levers, and road surfaces.

Motorcycle Pack

People who ride on motorcycles sometimes need to carry items with them. Motorcycles often have a small suitcaselike container attached behind the seat. Set out plastic lunch boxes for your children to play with. Encourage them to think of ways to attach the lunch boxes to their trikes.

Relay Race

Plan a relay race with your children. Line them up in two even groups and set out two trikes. Have the first child in each line get on a trike, ride to a designated area, ride back to the next person in their line, get off of the trike, and go to the end of the line. The next person in each line repeats the course. The group that finishes first is the winner.

Go Motorcycle

Sung to: "Kookaburra"

Motorcycle roaring down the street

With someone riding I'd like to meet.

Go, motorcycle,

Go, motorcycle.

How fun your life must be.

Motorcycle coming to a stop.

Look, everyone, it is a cop.

Go, motorcycle,

Go, motorcycle.

How fun your life must be.

Motorcycle cruising by the sea,

Look, everyone, the rider's me.

Go, motorcycle,

Go, motorcycle.

How fun my life must be.

Jean Warren

Listen to Me Roar

Sung to: "Jingle Bells"

Vroom, vroom, vroom,

Vroom, vroom, vroom,

Riding down the road.

Vroom, vroom, vroom,

Vroom, vroom, vroom,

Watch me as I go.

Helmet on, jacket tight,

Leather gloves and more.

I'm dressed to ride my motorbike.

Listen to me roar!

Vroom!

Jean Warren

Little Motorcycles

Five little motorcycles.

Making motors roar.

One runs out of gas

Now there are four.

Four little motorcycles

Going on a spree.

One pops a tire.

Now there are three.

Three little motorcycles

Racing on through.

One runs off the track.

Now there are two.

Two little motorcycles

Having lots of fun.

One falls behind.

Now there is one.

One little motorcycle

Knows the race is won.

It crosses the finish line.

Now there are none.

Carol Gnojewski

Flannelboard Fun

Using the illustrations to the right as your guide, cut five motorcycle shapes out of felt. Place them on a flannelboard as you recite the rhyme above.

Moving Vans

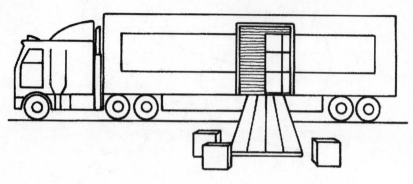

Someplace New

Show your children a picture of a moving van. Do any of them know what it is used for? Ask the children if any of their families have used a moving van for a long or short move. If you wish, talk about how moving means leaving one place and going to another. Discuss what it would be like to move someplace new, such as to a new town, a new school, or a new country.

Moving Van

Pretend that your wagon is a moving van, and you are the moving van driver. Encourage your children to help you load the van to move all the blocks, for example, "across town" (across the room). Let them be in charge. They will undoubtedly have their own ideas about how to "pack" the blocks. If you wish, have them decide where the blocks should be dumped or unloaded. This is a good way to engage the children's interest in cleanup time.

Moving Experts

Plan a field trip to a local moving, transport, or storage company. Have your children decide what they would like to learn from the trip, such as what types of trucks are used for big and small moves, and how to pack toys and other items so they don't break. If you wish, invite the children to pretend that you are moving your room across town. Make arrangements to view the variety of moving vans—some are small trailers, some are small trucks, and some are large trucks. Show the children how the large trucks use ramps or automated tailgates.

Packing Discovery

Set up a packing materials discovery center. Try collecting a variety of packing materials. These might include shredded paper, packing foam, packing peanuts, wrapping paper, tissue paper, bubble wrap, packing tape, newsprint (or newspaper), foam cushioning, shipping tags, brown shipping tape, and shipping labels, (If you wish, send letters home to parents asking for any packing materials they may have). Encourage the children to experiment with using these materials to pack unbreakable items and toys into small boxes.

The Art of Packing

Let the children use the packing materials you have gathered to make unique open-ended art creations. The following are a few projects you can suggest if your children want some direction.

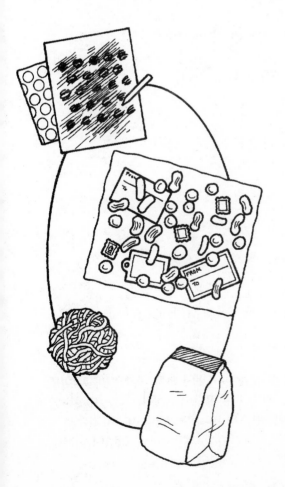

- **Bubble Wrap Rubbings**—Make rubbings of bubble wrap, packing foam, or corrugated cardboard.

- **Packing Peanut Collage**—Make collages on newspaper or other packing paper using different sizes, colors, and shapes of packing peanuts and foam pellets. Incorporate shipping tags, labels, and stamps.

- **Packing Tape Balls**—Roll or scrunch bubble wrap, packing paper, or foam cushioning into balls and secure with packing tape. Arrange tape sticky-side out around the ball, and cover with shredded paper, tissue paper, or packing peanuts.

- **Packing Pillows**—Stuff small paper or plastic bags with a variety of packing materials. Secure the opening with brown shipping tape.

Lots o' Boxes

Bring in several large packing boxes for your children to play with. If you can, try to locate dish packs, wardrobe cartons, and other special packing boxes. Invite the children to see how many of these they can "pack" into each box.

Street Address

Give your children adhesive address labels to put on small boxes and envelopes. Point out the numbers and words on them. Explain that these numbers and words make up your address. When you move, your address changes. Then sing the following song with your children to help them learn more about an address. Point to the different parts of an address as you sing.

My Address
Sung to: "Go In and Out the Window"

My home has a number,

My home has a number,

My home has a number,

It's part of my address.

My home is on a street,

My home is on a street,

My home is on a street,

It's part of my address.

Additional Verses: My home is in a city; My home is in a state, My home has a zip code.

Carol Gnojewski

Extension: Inform parents that you are learning about addresses. Invite them to bring in address labels for the children to use at school. Explain that this might be a good time to familiarize their children with the numbers and words of their own street address.

Garage Sale

Explain to your children that many people have garage sales before they move. At a garage sale, you gather up all of the items from your home that you don't want anymore and set them out on tables for people to look through and buy. Garage sales make moving easier because there is less to pack!

Set up a pretend garage sale in your room using toys, books, art supplies, dress-up clothes, and other small items. Mark all of the items with stickers that have numerals on them from 1 to 10. Give the children play coins or poker chips. Help the children count out the correct number of coins to "buy" the items of their choice.

Packed Snack

Pack individually wrapped snacks and/or drinks inside a large box. Secure the box with tape. Label the box with the word "Snack" and set it near your door. At snacktime, invite the children to figure out how to move the box into your snack area to open it. Help facilitate all safe suggestions. The children will enjoy the suspense of waiting to see what's in the box.

Racecars

On the Fast Track

Gather your children in a circle and invite them to tell you what they know about racecars. Then show them a picture or model of a racecar, and ask your children to describe it. Did they use the word *fast*? Talk about things that are fast with your children. What do they think of when they hear the word *fast*? Can they think of other words or expressions that mean the same thing as *fast*?

Built for Speed

Racecars are built very low to the ground, with powerful engines to make them speedy. Some racecars even have wings on the front and back of them to keep them from tipping over as they make fast turns around racetracks.

Provide your children with nature or transportation magazines. Have the children tear out pictures of fast animals or vehicles. Have the children arrange the pictures from the fastest to the slowest animal or vehicle. Let them explain their system. Accept all logical answers.

Racecar Numbers

Explain to your children that racecars have numbers painted on the sides of them so that racing officials can identify them. Then collect a small toy racecar for each of your children. Write numerals on dot stickers and place them, on the cars. One at a time, let the children choose a racecar. Ask each child to identify the number on his or her racing car. Then let the children pair up and race the cars on the floor.

Racing Flags

Many colors of flags are used in auto racing, but the most familiar one is the checkered flag. For each of your children, set out a piece of white construction paper and several 2-by-2-inch pieces of black construction paper. Let the children use the black squares to create their own patterns on the white flag.

Extension: Cover the children's checker-patterned creations with clear self-stick paper and use them as placemats during snacktime.

Lap Racer

Prepare a racetrack by marking off a large oval on the ground using chalk, rope, or masking tape. Then number small cards or slips of paper from 1 to 5. Make sure there are more cards than there are children in your group. Place all of the numbered cards inside a bicycle helmet. Invite one child at a time to be the Racer and to pick a card from the helmet. After identifying the number on the card, have the Racer run that number of laps around the track. Invite the rest of the group to count the laps each Racer runs. Encourage the Racer to make racing sounds, such as *vroom* and *zoom* as he or she pretends to race around the track.

Variation: Try this activity with riding toys.

Oval Track Art

One of the types of speedways that cars race on is the oval track. Cut an oval in the center of a piece of cardboard. Compare an oval to a circle. Explain that it is almost a circle, but stretched-out instead of round. Then let the children use the mat frame to trace ovals on sheets of construction paper. Provide racecar stickers, and invite the children to place the stickers on their oval tracks.

Extension: Show your children how to make ovals with their hands by holding their hands in front of them as if they were eating a sandwich. The shape they see when they look through the opening is an oval. Help your children look through their ovals to identify other oval shapes around your room.

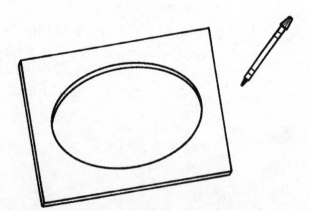

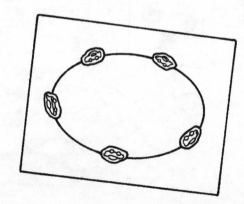

Racing Games

Enjoy some time outside with your children playing racing games. Before you start, make sure that you clearly mark the racing field, so that the children know where to start and where to end. Develop a system, such as blowing a whistle or dropping a flag, for letting your children know when to begin each race.

Here are some fun racing games to try.

- **Racecar and Spoon**—This is a variation of an egg and spoon race. Provide each racer with a large spoon and a small toy car. Have each child place the car inside his or her spoon. It will be a challenge for your children to balance their cars on the spoons as they walk as fast as they can to the finish line.

- **Speed Dresser**—For each player, provide a grocery sack filled with racing gear, such as gloves, helmets, oversize shoes, or oversize shirts or bodysuits. (You may need to limit how many racers can race at a time.) Place the sacks at your finish line. Have the racers run to the sacks, put on the clothes, and run back to the starting line as fast as they can in their racing clothes.

- **Rabbit and Turtle Race**—First, have a race where the children run as fast as rabbits. Then have the children run like turtles, or as slow as they can!

Hint: To take the edge out of the competitive aspect of racing, try focusing on the fun of each activity. Stress finishing, rather than winning. After each race, bring all the children together for a group hug, so everyone will feel like a winner.

Pit Stop

A pit is an area beside a racetrack where race drivers take their cars during a race when they need to be fixed or they are out of gas. Explain to your children that going into a pit during a race is called *making a pit stop*. Help your children make a pit stop outside in the play yard. Set up a table with tools, empty gas cans, a pitcher of water, and paper cups. Let your children refuel their trikes as needed.

Banana Racecar

Give each of your children a banana, a mandarin orange slice, and two toothpicks. Let the children use small plastic knives to cut two slices from each end of the banana to make wheels. Show them how to insert a toothpick through each end of the banana where they want the wheels to go. Have them carefully press the four banana wheels onto the four toothpick ends. Then help the children slice the top of the banana in a *V* shape for the driver's seat. Have them set the orange slice on the *V* for the driver's helmet.

Hint: Carefully supervise your children as they use the knives and toothpicks.

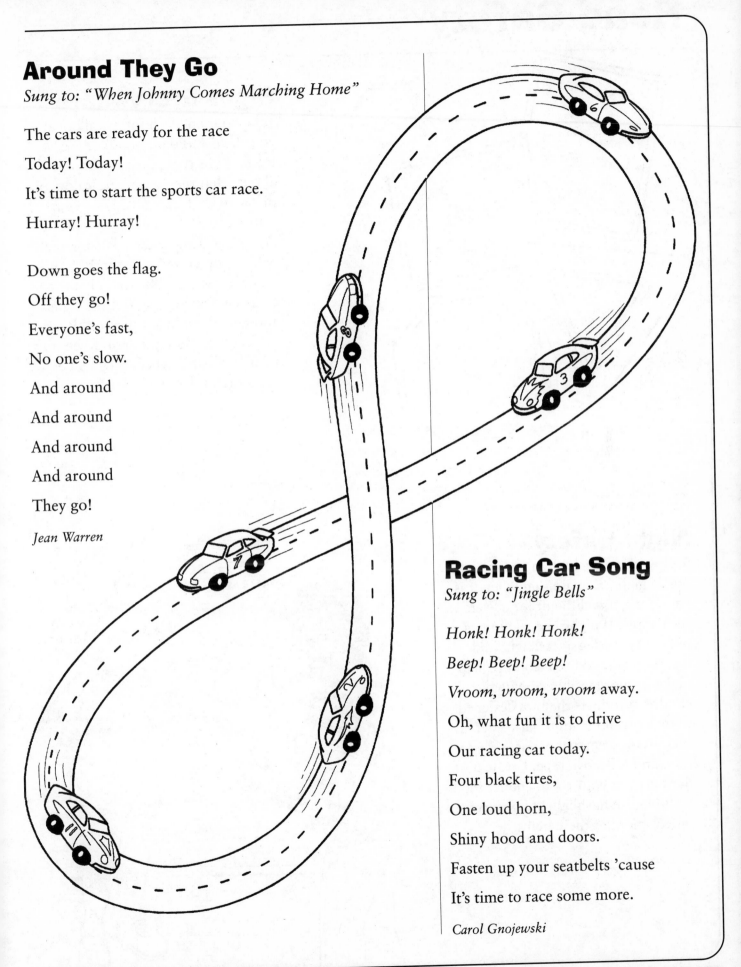

Around They Go

Sung to: "When Johnny Comes Marching Home"

The cars are ready for the race

Today! Today!

It's time to start the sports car race.

Hurray! Hurray!

Down goes the flag.

Off they go!

Everyone's fast,

No one's slow.

And around

And around

And around

And around

They go!

Jean Warren

Racing Car Song

Sung to: "Jingle Bells"

Honk! Honk! Honk!

Beep! Beep! Beep!

Vroom, *vroom, vroom* away.

Oh, what fun it is to drive

Our racing car today.

Four black tires,

One loud horn,

Shiny hood and doors.

Fasten up your seatbelts 'cause

It's time to race some more.

Carol Gnojewski

Road Safety

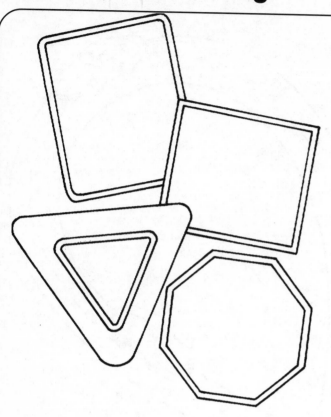

Signs Everywhere

Take your children for a walk near your facility. Point out all of the traffic signs that you see, and talk about what they mean. To follow up this activity, locate a copy of your state's driver's manual (available at a driver licensing office). The manual will have pictures of the traffic signs that are used in your state. Let the children help you cut out the signs and glue them in a notebook. Read the book to your children. Keep it in your book area where they will enjoy "reading" it by themselves.

Night Safety

Talk with your children about walking at night. Explain that when it is very dark, it is difficult for drivers to see people. If nighttime walking is necessary, taking a flashlight and wearing light-colored clothing helps make us more visible. Show your children products that are designed to make walking after dark safer, such fluorescent armbands, reflectors, and reflective tape. Create a dark area in your room and let the children use flashlights to observe one or more of these items.

Crossing the Street

Sung to: "Twinkle, Twinkle, Little Star"

Look both ways when you cross the street.
  (Look one way and then the other.)

Move your eyes before your feet.

Look around you near and far.
  (Look around room.)

Wait for roads to have no cars.

Look both ways when you cross a street.

Move your eyes before your feet.

Cross the street when the light is green.

Never on red or in-between.
  (Shake head side-to-side.)

Watch what other walkers do
  (Look around group.)

Hold someone's hand and stay with them, too.
  (Hold the hand of the person next to you.)

Cross the street when the light is green.

Never on red or in-between.

Carol Gnojewski

Street Scene

Create a pretend street scene on the floor of your room. Use black tape to designate roads. Invite your children to help you make the scene as realistic as possible by adding details such as signs, trees, sidewalks, and buildings. Then provide them with toy vehicles and small action figures. Encourage the children to use the action figures to show you how to cross the street safely.

Traffic Jam

Put masking tape on the floor to represent a four-way intersection. Have your children pretend to drive cars and trucks that are approaching the intersection from different directions. You play the traffic cop standing in the intersection (with a whistle around your neck, if possible). Invite your children to grip their "steering wheels" and make their engines *vroom* and their horns honk. Blow the whistle and motion one line of children across the intersection at a time. Let the children who cross the intersection get in the back of another line and approach you from a different direction.

Who Drives a Car With Flashing Lights?

Sung to: "She'll Be Coming Round the Mountain"

Look who drives a car with flashing lights on top,

And who keeps us safe and makes the traffic stop.

Look who stands so tall and proud,

And who blows a whistle loud.

Take a look and see our friend the traffic cop.

Diane Thom

Traffic Light Game

Gather three flashlights. Cover the front end of one flashlight with a piece of red cellophane, cover another with green cellophane, and cover the third flashlight with yellow cellophane. Invite your children to be cars and drive around the room as you sing the song below. When a color is called out, switch on the appropriate flashlight. Instruct your children to "drive" when the green light is shining, slow down when the yellow light is shining, and stop when the red light is shining.

Traffic Light Song
Sung to: "Ring Around the Rosie"

See the green light glowing,

See the traffic flowing.

Yellow light,

Red light,

Traffic, stop!

Bobbie Lee Wagman

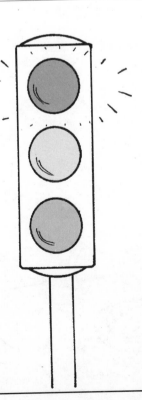

Safety Sign Spinner Game

Divide a clean round pizza board into eight to 12 pie sections. Stick a safety sign sticker on each section. (Safety sign stickers can be found at craft and teacher supply stores. Or simply draw on safety signs, including traffic signs.) Cut an arrow shape out of heavy cardboard and fasten it to the center of the pizza board with a metal paper fastener.

Gather your children in a circle. Let one child spin the arrow and identify the sign it lands on. Ask the child to tell you something about the sign. This is a good way to give the children an outlet for expressing their own ideas about safety. Continue until each child has had a turn.

Traffic Light Snacks

Give each of your children half of a hot dog bun. Let them spread on mayonnaise, if desired. Set out red pepperoni circles, yellow cheese circles, and green pickle circles. Have the children create "traffic lights" by arranging the red, yellow, and green circles in vertical rows on their hot dog buns.

Buckle Up

Collect adult-size elastic belts, or use pieces of wide elastic with magnets attached to the ends. Wrap the belts around the backs of several child-size chairs in your room. Rest the ends of the belts in the chair seats. Let your children have fun lining up the chairs to make cars. Have them buckle up before they start to "drive."

Seat Belt Song

Sung to: "The Muffin Man"

We have seat belts in our car.

We fasten them to go near or far.

We'll be as safe as we can be.

It's easy as 1-2-3.

Push the buckle in—snap it goes.

Now we're safe from head to toe.

We'll be as safe as we can be.

It's easy as 1-2-3.

Kathleen Hughes

Roads & Highways

Road Talk

Show your children pictures of the many types of roads that are available for vehicles to travel on. Discuss how some are wide and long, such as highways and freeways. In towns and cities, there are many types of roads, including streets, avenues, lanes, boulevards, and so on. Sometimes we have to pay to drive on certain roads, called *toll roads*.

Invite your children to build a system of roads in your play yard or sandbox for toy vehicle play. Encourage them to create some of the different types of roads you have discussed.

Road Collages

Give each of your children a large piece of construction paper. Set out glue and pieces of straight and curved construction paper strips. Let the children glue the different strips on their papers to create roads. Encourage them to fill their papers with straight roads, winding roads, and roads that cross or intersect.

Map Reading

Show your children a road map of your state or city. Talk briefly about how a driver "reads" a map. See if you can find your town, your facility, and other familiar landmarks on the map. What landmarks might the children include if they were making a map of your room or the area surrounding your facility?

Floor Map

Use masking tape to create a large road map on the floor. Make sure that the roads are wide enough for toy cars and trucks to travel on. If you wish, add details such as pictures of houses, stores, a park, and your facility. Invite the children to find more than one way to "drive" their vehicles to different locations on the road map.

Variation: Take this activity outside and make the road map large enough for use with your children's riding vehicles.

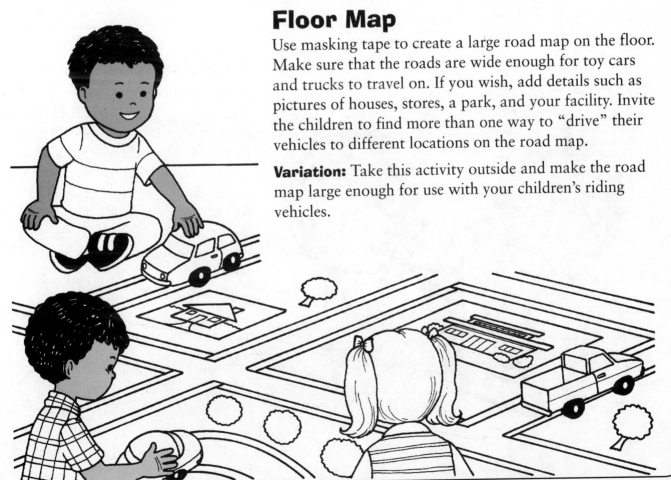

Paved Snack

Pavers are vehicles that help to make roads. They spread hot asphalt evenly across the ground. When the asphalt cools, the road is ready for cars and trucks to drive on. Provide each of your children with a piece of bread and a plastic knife. In the center of each bread slice, place a dollop of whipped cream cheese, peanut butter, jam, or butter. Encourage the children to use their knives like a paver to spread an even layer on their bread. Supervise children carefully when using sharp utensils.

Roll Away

Vehicles called rollers are used to flatten newly paved roads. They have large, wide steel wheels called *drums* that pack down the asphalt and make it smooth. Bring in a rolling pin for your children to use as a roller. Provide mounds of modeling dough, and encourage the children to use the "roller" to roll the dough out flat.

Sticky Road

Many roads are made out of asphalt, which is a black, sticky mixture of oil, rocks, and sand. Let your children go outdoors and mix up their own "asphalt." Provide dirt, water, sand, and pebbles. Encourage the children to use their "asphalt" to pave a road you mark off with tape.

Different Pavement

Explain to your children that roads can be made of asphalt or concrete. If possible, bring in pieces of asphalt and concrete for your children to explore. Or show pictures of roads or other structures made out of these two substances. How are they alike? How are they different? Go outside and look carefully at the roads near your facility. What kinds of pavements do they have?

Road Lines

Take your children outside to look at a road or highway near your facility. Point out how the road is marked off with solid white lines and dotted white lines. Have your children use white chalk to practice making solid or dotted lines on your blackboard or sidewalk.

Variation: Let the children use white chalk or crayons to draw solid or dotted lines on black construction paper.

Road Game

Create a road game out of an existing gameboard from an old board game such as Candyland or Monopoly (or make your own gameboard by marking off a trail of squares on a piece of posterboard). Make two photocopies of the Road Game Cards on page 117. Photocopy four sets of the number cards and two sets of the take- or lose-a-turn cards. Cut out the cards and cover them with clear self-stick paper. Mix up the cards and stack them so they are facing down. At each turn, a child selects one card. He or she must count and move the number of dots or follow the picture directions on each card. Instead of game pieces, let your children move small toy cars and trucks around the board.

Road Game Cards

Use with the activity on page 116.

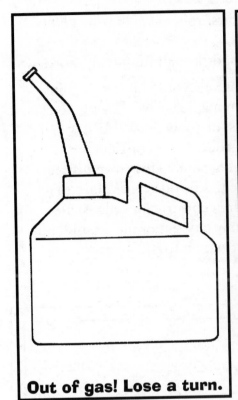

Out of gas! Lose a turn.

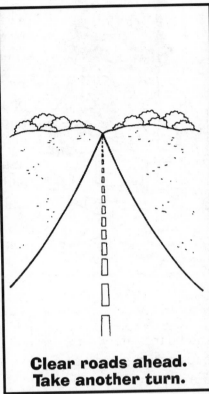

**Clear roads ahead.
Take another turn.**

Flat tire! Lose a turn.

Roller Skates & Skateboards

Where Would You Roll?

The first roller skates were adaptations of ice skates designed for transportation rather than sport.

Encourage your children to think of an imaginary world with no cars, buses, or subways. What if we all used roller skates or skateboards to get around? How would streets and cities be different? Have the children construct a roller-skate-friendly city out of blocks and other construction toys.

Safety Dress-up

Add a supply of roller skate and skateboard safety gear, such as helmets, kneepads, elbow pads, wrist guards, and gloves, to your dress-up area. Be sure to provide a mirror! Show your children how to adjust and position this equipment so it fits correctly. Then talk about what each piece is used for. (Helmets protect our head, knee and elbow pads protect our joints, and gloves or wrist guards protect the palm of our hands.) Ask your children what they think would happen if they fell while roller skating or skateboarding without wearing safety gear?

Our Roller Rink

Set aside space for a pretend roller rink in your facility. Invite your children to help you decide how big the skating area will be, and where people who are waiting to skate can sit and watch. Discuss other skating rules, such as appropriate dress and footgear (shoes or stocking feet), how many people can skate at one time, and which direction everyone should skate in. If you wish, let the children select music to skate to, and include songs for partner skates (have the partners hold hands while skating).

Have your children pretend to skate by gliding one foot at a time across the floor. Teach them fun skate moves like bending your knees as you skate or crossing one foot over the other to make turns. Or have your children attempt to skate backward. How slow can your children skate? How fast?

Hint: Be sure to have at least one adult supervising in the skating area at all times.

Roller Romp

The earliest roller skates were nothing more than wooden spools or metal wheels nailed into wood strips and fastened onto boots or shoes. Now special wheels are already attached to skating boots. Let any child who wishes try on a pair of real or in-line roller skates. Point out how much heavier skates are than normal shoes. What makes them heavier? Help your children keep their balance by holding their hands while they attempt to stand up and move forward on skates.

Hint: Inexpensive slip-on roller skates with velcro attachments can be purchased at most toy stores or discount drugstores. Consider purchasing a pair or more of these skates for indoor/outdoor play.

Different Skates

Gather different types of skates including in-line skates (commonly called Rollerblades™), skateboards, and regular quad (four-wheel) roller skates. Ask parents and staff to bring in skates from home, or invest in some used skates from thrift stores or garage sales. Divide your children into groups of twos or threes and give each group a skate. Have the children discuss the features that make them alike and different.

Skate Science

Let your children count the number of wheels on the skating equipment you have on hand. What do they think would happen if roller skates and skateboards had fewer wheels? More wheels? If you wish, try removing or adding wheels to old equipment (ask your local skate shop for tools and how-to information).

Skateboard Scoot

Mark a start and stop line on the floor or the sidewalk with masking tape. One at a time let your children sit on a skateboard and scoot from one end to the other. Practice safe skateboarding by providing a helmet for your children to wear as they ride. (You may want to plan ahead and have the children bring helmets from home so that you don't waste time taking off and putting on helmets.)

Encourage them to keep their hands away from the wheels to prevent pinched fingers.

Hint: Glue grip tape to the top of the board to increase traction.

Variation: Let younger children use the skateboard to roll stuffed animals across the floor.

Let's Roll

Sung to: "A-Tisket, A-Tasket"

Let's roll let's ride,

Let's take a longer stride.

Keep on rolling, keep on going,

Take me for a ride.

Use one foot to push off,

Then take a rest and glide.

Keep on rolling, keep on going,

Take me for a ride.

Connie R. Ion

Skate Wagon

Tie a piece of string around the front *wheel assembly* of a skateboard to make a wagonlike pull toy. Encourage your children to use the Skate Wagon during play or cleanup times to transport small items, such as blocks, books, or dolls, from one area of the room to another.

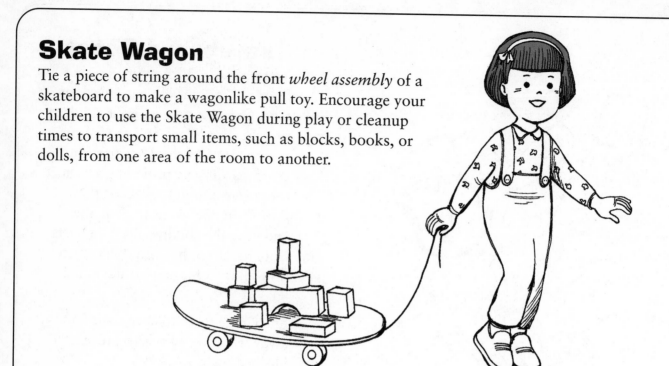

Skateboard Shuffle

Cut skateboard-shaped ovals out of cardboard for each of your children. Show them how to stand on their "skateboards" with one foot in front of the other. Model how to hold your arms out to the sides to stay balanced as you lean from one side to the other. Explain that a skateboard will turn in the direction that you lean. This is the way you steer it to make it go where you want it to go. Help the children balance and lean on their boards. Have them try other movements, such as keeping one foot on the skateboard while the other is in the air or on the ground, hopping on and off, and jumping up and down with both feet on the skateboard. Play some lively music while they practice these fun skateboarding moves.

Variation: Try this activity with boogie boards, surfboards, or kickboards.

Extension: Periodically, stop the music and have the children "freeze" in a funny position. Can they think up a different pose each time? Take pictures while they are "frozen" and share them with the parents or use them for a skateboard bulletin board.

Paint the Deck

The *deck* of a skateboard is the plywood board that the wheels are attached to. The top of the deck is covered with a rough, sandpaperlike texture to keep skateboarders from slipping off. The bottom of the deck is usually very smooth. Skateboarders often personalize the bottom of the deck by painting on designs or covering it with stickers. Let your children feel the difference between the rough deck top and the smooth deck bottom. Then set out art supplies, including grip tape or sandpaper, and let the children decorate the cardboard skateboard shapes they used for the Skateboard Shuffle. Help them make one side of their board smooth and the other side rough.

Skateboard Sticks

Turn craft sticks into skateboards. The children can decorate them with markers and then use them for creative play with a road mat and some action figures. Tape butcher paper to a table, and let the children make their own road mat by drawing lines for roads.

Snack Rollers

Use an open-face oblong hoagie roll to make a skateboard pizza. Top with pizza sauce and grated veggies such as carrots or zucchini. Add cheese and then heat until it melts. For wheels, attach olives to the bottom of the roll with toothpicks.

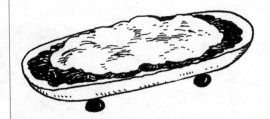

Trucks

If I Were a Truck

Talk about trucks with your children. Where can you find trucks? What do they carry? See how many different types of trucks your children can name. Then encourage the children to complete the following sentences. Older children may enjoy illustrating their responses.

If I were a truck,

I'd be a _____ truck

and I'd carry_____.

Truck Walk

Take your children for a walk to discover the different kinds of trucks that can be found in your area. (You may be surprised at the number of trucks you see.) What is each truck used for? How are the trucks the same? How are they different?

Extension: Invite your children to dictate a group story about their walk.

I'm a Truck

Sung to: "This Old Man"

I'm a truck, a ten-ton truck.

I cross the country loaded with stuff.

I am big and powerful and strong.

Hop in my cab and ride along.

Carol Gnojewski

Ten-Ton Truck

The weight of trucks is measured by the ton. Some trucks can pull as much as five times more than they weigh. Truck drivers often must stop and weigh their trucks at weigh stations as they travel across state lines.

Set up a weigh station in your room. Use a poster board to make a weight chart, and bring in a floor scale. One at a time, have your children stand on the scale. Record each child's weight on the weight chart. Next, have the children carry something and be weighed again. Write down the new weight next to the original weight. Continue with new loads if interest lasts. Leave the scale in block area.

Name	Weight	Weight with book
Lily		
Sam		
Joshua		
Lionel		
David		
Maddie		
Alyssa		
Eleanor		
Jake		

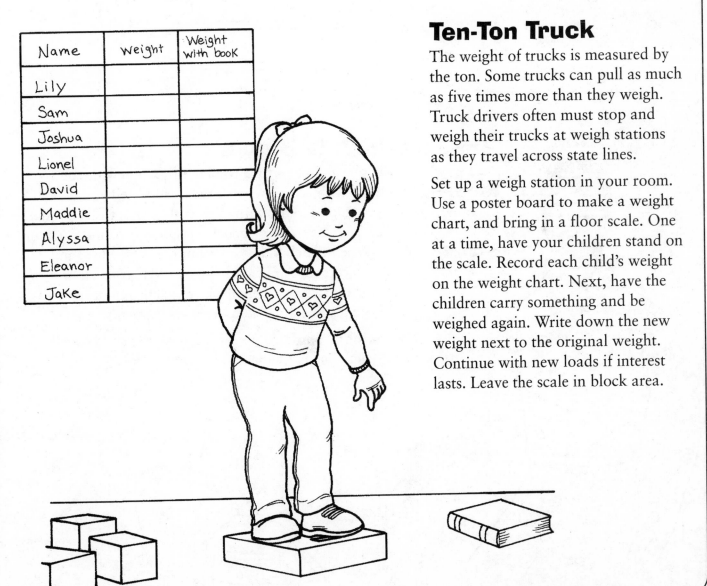

Building Trucks

Cut out a variety of basic shapes, such as squares, circles, triangles, and rectangles, from heavy paper. Let your children use these shapes to form their own truck shapes. Invite them to glue their trucks onto construction paper. If you wish, use the truck pictures to decorate a bulletin board.

Variation: Instead of using paper shapes, have the children work together to build a group truck out of Lincoln Logs, wooden blocks, or other play construction materials.

Which Is Bigger?

Invite one child at a time to play this game with you. Name two objects. Then ask the child to tell you which object is bigger. Start with objects that aren't very similar in size, such as truck or pencil, truck or cup, and truck or cake. When the child becomes familiar with this game, name objects that are closer in size, such as truck or house and truck or elephant. Encourage him or her to ask similar questions for you to answer.

Variation: Name two objects and ask the child to tell you which one is smaller.

Truck Stops

Truck stops are restaurants near highways that are open all night for truck drivers and other people who need to rest, relax, and eat while traveling. People who wait tables at truck stops often use fun descriptions when giving an order to the cook. For example, they may call two eggs on toast *Adam and Eve on a raft*. A small order of chocolate milk might be called a *small brown cow*.

Encourage your children to make up silly names for their favorite food or snacks, such as *white mud* for mashed potatoes or *box of bugs* for prepackaged raisins. If you wish, call these foods by their new names at snacktime.

Many Wheeler

Show your children pictures of different types of large trucks (see book list on page 129). Explain that these trucks have different numbers of wheels depending on their size and the size of the trailers they pull. Cut several small circles out of black felt for truck wheels. Then cut a wheel-less truck shape from a different color of felt (or photocopy one of the Truck Cards on pages 130–131 and back it with felt or flannel, making sure to cut off any existing wheels).

Place the truck shape on a flannelboard. Invite one child at a time to use the felt wheels to make different-wheeled vehicles. For example, you might ask one child to make you a three-wheeler truck. You might ask another child to make a six-wheeler or a ten-wheeler.

Monster Truck Creations

In a small container, collect spare parts from broken toys, especially from toy cars and trucks. When you have gathered a sufficient amount of odds and ends, let your children use them to make their own monster trucks.

Explain that monster trucks are trucks that have extra parts added to them, such as special engines, huge wheels, and rollover bars that help them climb over anything (including other trucks and cars). They are also used to race through mud and dirt. Help each child use modeling dough to attach a few odds and ends to one of the toy trucks you have available or one they bring from home.

Extension: Monster trucks have powerful racing names such as Crusher, Black Magic, and Blue Thunder. Encourage your children to think of special names for their truck creations.

Keep on Truckin'

"Keep on Truckin'" is a famous bumper sticker slogan. Bring in bumper stickers for your children to look at. Read the stickers and talk about what they mean. Then set out plain white address or file labels and art supplies such as markers, crayons, and paints. If you wish, provide a small truck stamp and stamp pad. Let your children use these materials to make bumper stickers for their toy trucks or riding vehicles. Encourage older preschoolers to combine words (or letters) and pictures on their stickers.

Truck Cards

Use the patterns on pages 130–131 to make matching games for your children. Make two photocopies of each page and color the pictures if you wish. Cover the pages with clear self-stick paper and then cut into quarters to make cards. Let your children use the cards to play concentration and other matching games.

Truck Books

Introduce your children to these and other books about trucks and the work they do.

Big Book of Real Trucks, Walter Retan, Illus. by Richard Courtney. Grosset & Dunlap, 1987.

Make Way for Trucks, Gail Herman, Illus. by Christopher Santoro. Random House, 1990.

Mighty Machines Big Rig, Caroline Bingham, Illus. by Ellis Nadler, Photo. by Richard Leeney. Dorling Kindersley, 1996.

Tonka Big Book of Trucks, Patricia Relf, Illus. by Thomas LaPadula. Scholastic, 1996.

Trucks, Byron Barton. Crowell, 1986.

Trucks, Anne Rockwell. Dutton, 1984.

Trucks You Can Count On, Doug Magee. Dodd, Mead, 1985.

Truck Cards Patterns

Use with the activity on page 129.

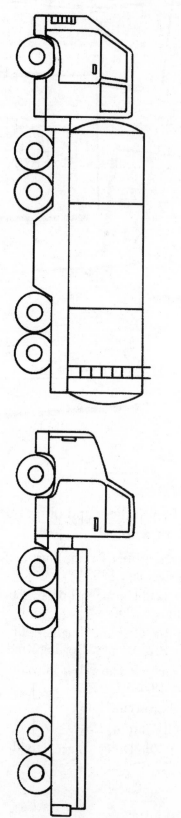

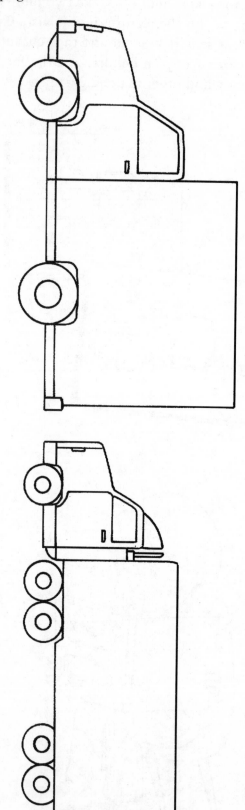

Truck Cards Patterns

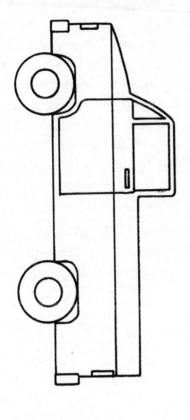

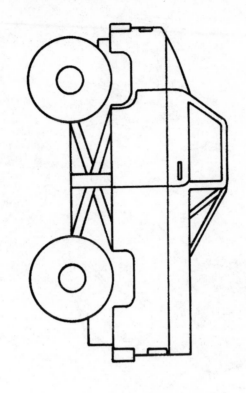

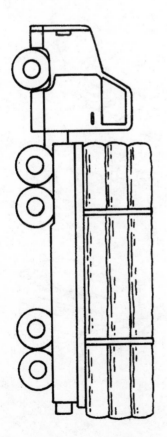

Wagons & Carts

Wagons & Carts

Bring in a wagon and a small shopping cart. Discuss how both of these items are hand-operated. Can your children think of other cartlike items that people use? Ideas include baby buggies, strollers, wheelbarrows, library carts, food carts, etc. Decide with your children which of these items are pushed and which are pulled, or both.

Note: More information on wagons and carts can be found in the Farm Vehicles unit on pages 72–77.

Push and Pull Song
Sung to: "Go In and Out the Window"

I can pull my wagon,
   (Pretend to pull a wagon around the room.)

I can pull my wagon,

I can pull my wagon

All around the town.

I can push my cart,
   (Pretend to push a cart around the room.)

I can push my cart,

I can push my cart

All around the town.

Have your children replace other items that can be pulled or pushed for *wagon* and *cart*.

Carol Gnojewski

Wagon Course

Arrange stuffed animals or other objects along the floor to form a simple obstacle course. Let your children take turns pulling a wagon through the course. As they grow more confident, decrease the space between the objects. Invite them to put the objects in the wagon on the final trip.

Wagon Panels

Cut two long, narrow rectangles out of cardboard. Let your children decorate the rectangles to look like the sides of a fire engine, a circus wagon, a food cart, or another type of wagon or cart. Attach the rectangles to the sides of a wagon using strong tape. Let your children use the paneled wagon in your riding-toy area.

Wagon Art

Cut paper to fit inside a wagon. Put the paper in the wagon along with crayons, chalk, or colored pencils. Set the wagon outside. Invite one child at a time to take the wagon to a place in the yard. Encourage the child to create art on the paper in the wagon by bending over the side of the wagon or crawling into it. Let the child move the wagon to as many places as he or she wants.

Shopping Cart

Let your children help you set up one section of your room as a store. Have the children help you stack a variety of toys and other items on shelves and on top of boxes for the store's displays. Let one child at a time be a shopper and pull a wagon through the store as a shopping cart. After the child is done "shopping," help him or her put the items back on the shelves. Then let another child go shopping.

Play Wagon

Punch a hole in the edge of a large foil pan. Put one end of a ribbon through the hole and tie it. Make a loop handle with the other end of the ribbon. Let one of your children fill the pan with items, hold onto the ribbon, and pull the pan around the room. Make several pull toys for your children to use as mini-wagons and -carts.

Group Stroll

Talk about what a baby stroller is and what it's used for. Ask the children if they remember riding in a stroller when they were babies. Do they remember what their baby strollers looked like? Then invite your children to help you round up all of the dolls and stuffed animals in your room. Put the dolls and animals in doll strollers, baby strollers, or wagons and go outside for a group stroll. Let the children take turns pushing the strollers.

Wheelbarrow Movement

Show your children a picture of a wheelbarrow. Then invite one of your children to pretend to be a wheelbarrow and lie down with his or her stomach to the floor. Then lift the child up by his or her ankles. Move forward, encouraging the child to walk on his or her hands. Under your supervision, let older preschoolers pair off and try this movement together.

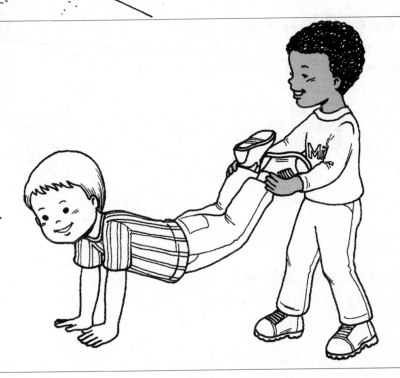

Wagon Table

Stabilize a wagon or cart by placing heavy books, such as phone books, behind the wheels. Let the children use the wagon as a table for board games, card games, or block play. At snacktime, line the wagon with paper towels. Set snack food in the center of the wagon, and let the children sit around the wagon to eat their snack.

Wheels

Counting Wheels

Collect various types of toys that have wheels, such as cars, trucks, wheelbarrows, trikes, and wagons. Invite your children to sit with you. Encourage them to touch and examine the wheels on the toys. Then together count the number of wheels on each toy.

Wheel Shapes

Bring in a shape sorter with a variety of shapes such as triangles, squares, diamonds, rectangles, circles, stars, and ovals. Have the children try to roll each shape. Discuss which shapes make the best wheels.

Wheel Puzzles

Wheels come in many different sizes, from small toy wagon wheels to large tractor wheels. Find pictures of wheeled vehicles in magazines and catalogs. Or use the patterns on pages 140–141. Point out the different sizes of wheels on these vehicles. Talk about why some wheels might need to be bigger than others. Then use scissors to cut out the wheels. Have the children complete the picture by adding on the appropriate wheels.

Hint: Cover the wheels and vehicles with clear self-stick paper, and store them separately in resealable plastic bags for future play.

Extension: Take a field trip to a local tire store or service station garage to see wheels of different sizes firsthand.

Story Wheel

Gather your children in a circle. Begin to tell a story (a story about wheels would be fun!). Roll a wheeled toy vehicle to one of your children. Encourage that child to add to the story before rolling the toy to someone else.

Wheel Rolling

Pair off your children and have one child pretend to be a wheel and roll across the floor, while the other gently guides the rolling child and keeps him or her from rolling into someone else. Have the children change places frequently.

Wheels Around Town

Sung to: "The Wheels on the Bus"

The wheels on the bus go round and round,

Round and round,

Round and round.

The wheels on the bus go round and round,

All through the town.

Additional verses: Substitute other wheeled vehicles for *bus*.

Have your children roll their hands in a circle whenever they sing the word *round*.

Traditional

Snack on Wheels

Provide snack foods that are naturally round, such as round crackers, wagon wheel pasta, cheese wheels or balls, and oranges. Place the snacks on a rolling cart, and wheel them to the table to serve.

Wheels and Axles

Show your children a toy car or truck. Point out that the wheels are attached to a bar called an *axle*. Collect rod-shaped materials such as sticks, craft sticks, dowels, Lincoln Logs, plastic tubing, and unsharpened pencils. Place these items in one basket. Collect wheel-shaped materials such as large metal washers, plastic rings, plastic-foam rings, hot rollers, and large macramé beads. Place these items in another basket. Encourage the children to make wheel and axle creations using the items from both baskets.

Variation: Do this activity with snack items such as pretzel rods and dried fruit rings. Let the children eat what they build.

Steering Wheels

Cut a steering wheel shape out of a piece of cardboard. Provide your children with magazines and catalogs that have a variety of vehicles in them. Have each child cut out a different vehicle and bring it to your circle. Show the children your steering wheel. Explain to them that a steering wheel is a wheel that is used to move or steer many different vehicles. Go around the circle and have each of the children hold up their vehicle picture. Does it have a steering wheel? If you wish, let the children make a group steering wheel collage by gluing the vehicles with steering wheels onto the cardboard steering wheel shape.

Wheel Puzzle Patterns

Use with the activity on page 136.

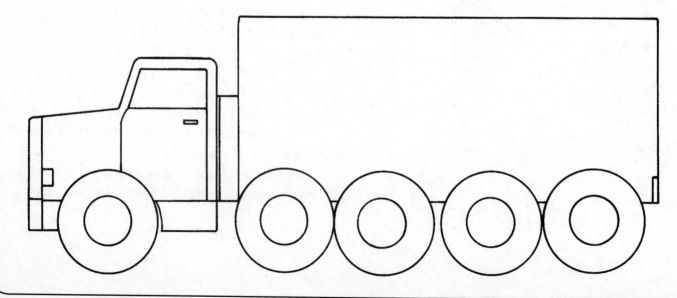

Wheel Puzzle Patterns

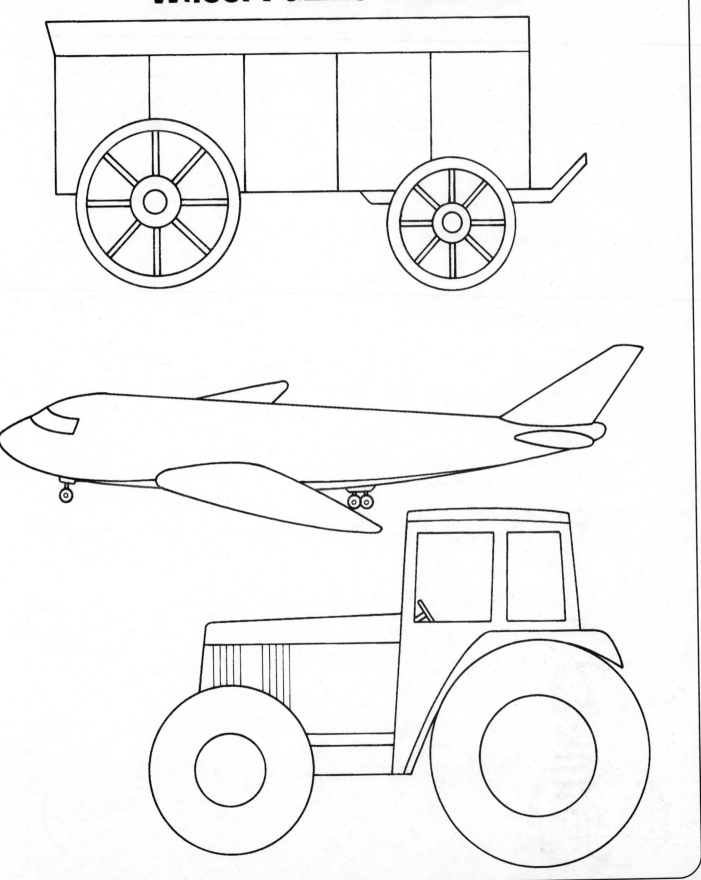

In the Air

Airplanes

Plenty of Planes

Planes are exciting because their highway is the sky. They give us a bird's-eye view of our cities and towns as they travel faster and farther than any other type of transportation.

There are many different kinds of planes.

Check your local library for books about airplanes, such as *The Story of Aviation*, edited by Ray Bonds (Barnes & Noble Inc., 1997). Show your children pictures of propeller planes, pontoon planes, biplanes, passenger jets, and fighter jets. Explain that propeller airplanes can land on short runways and are used for many things, including fighting forest fires and keeping track of storms. Pontoon planes can land on water and snow. Biplanes have two wings, which gives extra lift so they do not have to travel fast to stay in the air. Passenger jets travel fast and are used to carry people all over the world. Fighter jets are even faster. Most of them can land on aircraft carriers, which are large ships with flat decks that serve as runways.

Did You Ever See an Airplane?

Sung to: "Did You Ever See a Lassie?"

Did you ever see an airplane,

An airplane, an airplane?

Did you ever see an airplane

Way up in the sky?

There are prop planes and jet planes

And gliders and seaplanes.

Did you ever see an airplane

Way up in the sky?

Judith Taylor Burtchet

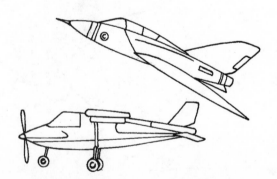

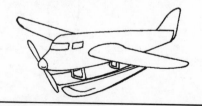

Just Plane Fun

Fill a sensory tub with cotton balls. Then set out small toy airplanes. Your children will have fun flying the toy planes through the clouds.

Variation: Fill the tub with water. Have the children pretend that the toy planes are seaplanes. Let them make takeoffs and landings in the water.

Head in the Clouds

Make a pretend sky by hanging blue or white crepe-paper streamers in a corner of your room. Cut the strips so they are long enough to dangle just within reach of your smallest child. Encourage the children to reach up and fly their toy planes through the paper "sky." Or let the children pretend they are airplanes. Challenge them to fly up into your sky.

Make a Plane

Cut out the patterns on page 151. For each of your children, trace the large and small wing patterns onto thin cardboard. Trace the airplane body (*fuselage*) pattern onto pieces of corrugated cardboard. (This is important so the wings stay level.) Cut out the parts and draw in the solid center lines on the wings. Use a craft knife to make two slits in each fuselage, as indicated by the dotted lines. Gently bend the large wings so they match the curve of the large slits. Show your children how to insert the wings in the slits so the wings' center line is in the exact center of the airplanes. Then have your children insert and center the back wings in the notched slit in the back. Tape two dimes to the front of each plane, one on either side of the nose. Let your children make their airplanes soar!

Hint: If an airplane stalls, move the main wing back. If it nosedives, move the main wing forward.

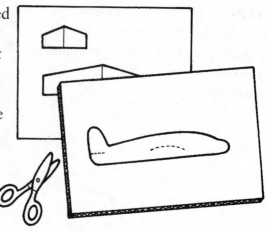

Airplane Art

Cut simple airplane shapes out of various colors of construction paper and let your children glue them onto blue paper. Have each child dip a cotton ball into white paint and dab it around (or on top of) their airplane for clouds.

If I Were a Plane

Bring in a large toy plane or airplane model. Name the different airplane parts for your children. Point out the nose, airplane body (fuselage), main wings, back wings, and tail. Then use this opportunity to review body parts with your children. Have your children decide where their nose, wings, and tail would be if they were an airplane. As you name a plane part, have them point to their corresponding body part.

What Can It Be?

Sung to: "Up on the Housetop"

What can it be that has a nose,

But stands on wheels instead of toes,

With two wings that never flap

And a tail that never wags back?

Won't you play this guessing game?

What can it be? It's an airplane!

Airplanes have wings, a tail, and a nose —

But they have wheels instead of toes!

Durby Peterson

All Clear for Takeoff

On a sunny day, take your children outdoors to an open area. Sing the following song and invite them to pretend that they are airplanes preparing for takeoff. Have them stand still, with arms outstretched for wings, until you say, "All clear for takeoff!" Then let them run and pretend to take off, soaring this way and that as they tilt their wings. Finally, have them come in for a landing.

My Airplane

Sung to: "If You're Happy and You Know It"

Oh, my airplane is a lot of fun to fly.

I can't wait to zoom around up in the sky.

Down the runway I go fast,

Climbing in the air at last.

Oh, my airplane is a lot of fun to fly.

Durby Peterson

Airliner Diner

Find a TV dinner tray for each of your children. On each tray place a snack such as crackers, vegetable sticks, dried fruit, and a drink. Then let your children help you line up chairs in rows to represent a large airplane cabin. Invite your children to sit in the chairs and pretend they are passengers on a jet airliner. Pretend to be the flight attendant who serves them their in-flight snack. Your children will enjoy holding the tray on their lap while they eat.

Home Is a Hangar

Explain to your children that planes are often parked in big garages called *hangars*. Collect an assortment of five toy airplanes; write the numerals 1 to 5 on stickers and attach them to the airplanes. Tape a long piece of butcher paper to the floor for a runway. Near the end of the runway, draw five rectangles for hangars. Number the hangars from 1 to 5 by drawing corresponding sets of dots. Let your children take turns making the airplanes land on the runway and park in the matching-numbered hangars.

Flying Machine

The first airplane to fly under its own power was Flyer, a flying machine built by Orville and Wilbur Wright, known as the Wright brothers. The Wright brothers experimented with gliders that were lifted by the wind. Flyer was a glider with a small engine attached to it that turned two propellers.

Show your children a picture of Flyer along with a picture or model of a modern passenger plane. How are the planes the same? How are they different? Guide their responses with question such as, "Which plane would be the most comfortable to fly in? Which plane would be the loudest? Which plane could carry our whole group? Which one would you like to fly in? Why?"

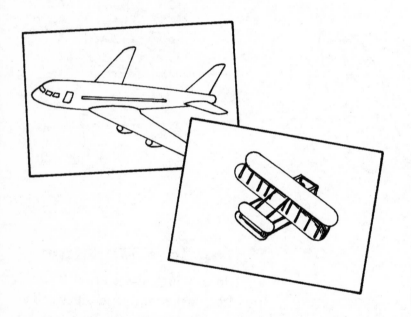

Go the Distance

Take your children outdoors and mark off a distance of 120 feet to show how far the Wright brothers' plane flew on its historic first flight. Give each of the children a paper airplane (or use the gliders from the Make a Plane activity on page 146). Have the children line up and throw their airplanes one at a time. Mark off the distance of each flight. Together with your group, use a tape measure to find out exactly how far each plane flew.

Flyer Really Flew

On December 17, 1903, the Wright brothers and Flyer made the first recorded flight in a small North Carolina town called Kitty Hawk. Kitty Hawk is near the coast of the Atlantic Ocean. It is a very windy place. The wind and Flyer's small engine helped keep Flyer in the air for 12 seconds.

Have your children pretend to be Flyer. As they fly around your room or play yard, help the children count to 12. Invite them to see how far they can fly before you reach the count of 12.

Airplane Pattern

Use with the activity on page 146.

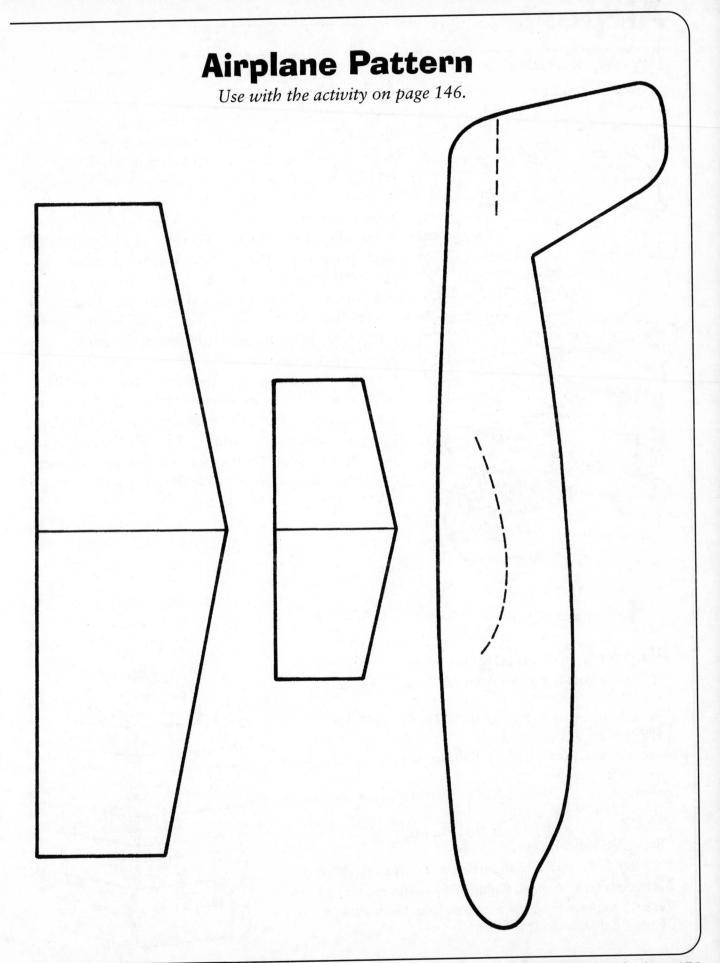

Airport

Our Airport

Invite your children to help you set up an airport in the home-life area. Help them think about what an airport is like by reading them related books or providing them with pictures. Talk about some of your own experiences in airports, and encourage the children to relate any experiences they may have had. Then help the children make a list of the equipment they want their airport to have. Guide their thinking by asking them questions. How many airplanes should it have? How many runways will you need? Does it have a ticket booth or control tower? Will it include a store for buying small items to read or eat on the plane? Will there be a place for luggage? What about a souvenir stand? Encourage them to come up with questions of their own. Together, think of ways to find out the answers. Perhaps you could invite a flight attendant, pilot, or airline employee to talk to the children and explain what they do. Help the children come up with ideas for making or collecting the items that they will need to complete their airport.

Airport Reading

Check your local library for these and other books about airports.

The Airport, Stuart A. Kallen. ABDO Publishing Company, 1997.

At the Airport, Marilyn Miller. Raintree Steck-Vaughn Publishers, 1996.

A Busy Day at the Airport, Phillipe Dupasquier. Candlewick Press, 1996.

Jonathan Goes to the Airport, Susan K. Baggette. The Brookfield Reader, 1998.

Let's Build an Airport, Kath Mellentin. Zero to Ten, 1998.

Let's Explore the Airport, Random House Incorporated, 1996.

Let's Go to the Airport, Barbara Bazaldua. Golden Books Family Entertainment, 1998.

Airport Field Trip

Plan a field trip to the airport with your children. Many airports offer organized tours. Before you go, ask your children to brainstorm a list of things you might see on your trip. Write the list on a chalkboard or large sheet of butcher paper. After you return, look over the list. Were there any surprises? Add any new discoveries to your list.

Pretend Trip

Plan a pretend trip with your group. First, bring in travel brochures and decide as a group where you would like to go. Then make airplane tickets for everyone out of different colors of construction paper. Line up chairs in rows for a plane ride, and tape pieces of construction paper in corresponding colors to each chair. Have each child find his or her seat according to the color of the ticket. Once everyone has a seat, ask your children to pretend to buckle up for the flight. Invite one child to be a flight attendant and hand out a packaged snack to all of the "passengers," If you wish, assume the role of pilot and talk your children through a takeoff and landing.

Extension: After the airplane ride, set up a discovery table with items the children might see or find at their destination. Include art supplies with these items and let the children use their imagination to make something to take home as a souvenir.

Airport Check

Your children may have witnessed a security check at the airport, or walked through a metal detector. Gather your children in a circle and explain that you are going to do a check of their pockets. (If a child doesn't have pockets, do a check of his or her shoes—feet and toes will be inside— or coat pockets.) Then pass around a small basket. One at a time, have each child empty the contents of his or her pockets into the basket. Let the child hold up each item, identify it, and tell the group something about it, such as what it is used for, what it is made of, or how it got there.

Extension: Talk with older preschoolers about things that are safe and unsafe to put in your pocket or bring to school.

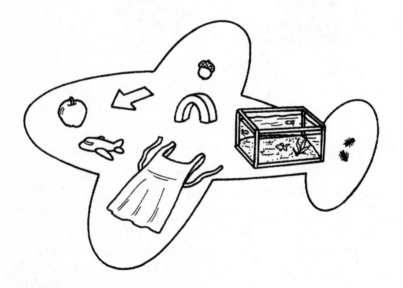

A Is for Airplane

Cut a large airplane shape out of butcher paper and label it with the letter A. Place the shape on the floor along with items that begin with A. Explain to your children that the airplane has to be loaded with A items before it can take off. Let the children take turns choosing an item, naming it, and placing it on the airplane shape. When the airplane is fully loaded, name all the A items with the group.

Departure

Numbers are important in an airport. You have to know the number of your plane, the number of the gate your plane leaves from, and the time of your flight. Give each of your children a number. Tell the children that their number represents their *departure* time, or the time their plane will leave. Rotate the hands on a toy clock or number spinner. When the big hand of the clock lands on a child's number, have that child identify his or her number. Then it's time for that child to "fly" to another area of your room for free play.

Pack a Suitcase

Bring in suitcases, duffel bags, or garment bags and have your children pack them for a trip to someplace far away. Provide the children with dress-up clothes. Show the children how to fold the dress-up clothes to fit inside the suitcases.

Extension: Talk with your children about other items besides clothes that are fun or essential to take with you on a plane trip.

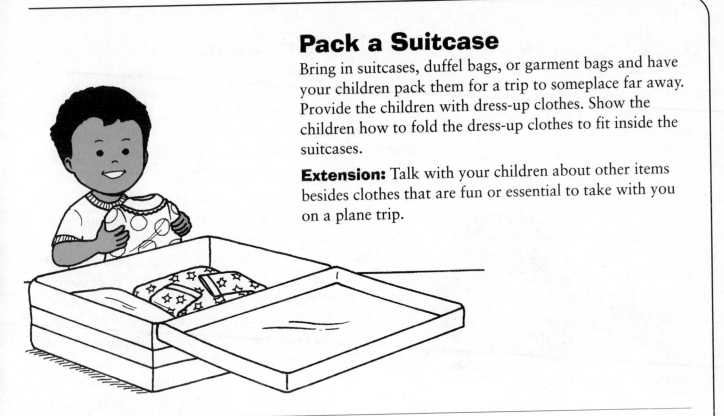

Baggage Claim Game

Cut matching sets of squares out of different colors of construction paper. Make sure there are only two squares per color, and one square total for each of your children. Punch a hole in the top of one set of squares and thread yarn through the holes to make color tags or necklaces. Then divide your children into two groups. Give each child in the first group a color tag. Have the children in the first group place the tags around their neck and form a circle. Invite them to pretend that they are suitcases and bags on a luggage carousel. Pretend to turn on the luggage carousel by pressing an imaginary button, and have the "luggage" slowly walk around the circle.

Invite the children in the other group to pretend that they are travelers claiming their luggage. Give each child one of the remaining squares. Have the "travelers" stand outside the circle and watch for the "luggage" that matches their color square. When a match is sighted, the traveler should catch up to his "luggage" in the circle and hold the person by the hand. Matched "travelers" and "luggage" should then leave the circle. When all pairs are matched, let the children switch tags and roles.

Variation: For a simplified version of this game, give all of the children tags and have them search around the room for their matching partner.

Moving Sidewalks

Did your children know that some escalators move people forward instead of up and down? These forward-moving escalators are called *moving sidewalks*, because they are flat instead of having steps. Moving sidewalks are often found in airports. They help people quickly move themselves and their luggage to and from their planes.

Make a moving sidewalk for your group's small toy people and action figures using the lid of a long rectangular gift box or other large rectangular lidded container. Cut two horizontal slits in the top of the box, one on either end of the lid. Thread a wide ribbon or long, heavy paper strip through the slits and tape or staple the ends loosely together. (You may need to trim the ends of the ribbon or paper before you tape them.) Show your children how to reach under the box and pull the ribbon toward them so it moves the ribbon steadily through the slits. (Widen the slits as needed to allow the ribbon to move freely.) Point out that half of the ribbon is underneath the box and half the ribbon is showing above the box at any given time. Have the children use the moving sidewalk to move their small action figures from one end of the box to the other.

Airport Dress-up

The following are suggestions for dress-up items to collect or make for your children's airport play.

🛩 **Air Traffic Controller dress-up**—headphones, radio, binoculars

🛩 **Flight Attendant dress-up**—trays, pillows, blankets, magazines, emergency procedures rebus cards, air sickness bags, oxygen masks

🛩 **Ground Crew dress-up**—flags, flashlights, headphones, work gloves

🛩 **Passenger dress-up**—luggage, camera, airplane ticket, baggage-claim tags

🛩 **Pilot dress-up**—pilot hat, wing badge, headphones, flight log book

Air Traffic Control Game

Using tape or chalk, mark off a wide runway on the floor of your room. Have your children line up across one end of the runway and pretend to be airplanes while you stand at the opposite end of the runway and pretend to be an air traffic controller. Explain to the children that airplane pilots must carefully follow the directions given to them by air traffic controllers during takeoffs and landings.

Then give the "airplanes" instructions such as, "Airplanes, skip forward three times. Airplanes, take two tiny steps backward. Hop forward five times." Continue until the children reach your end of the runway. If you wish, let the children take turns being air traffic controllers.

Extension: To challenge older preschoolers, make several narrow runways and mark them with a specific number, color, or shape. Make sure there is only one child per runway. Give each "airplane" individual instructions. For instance, you might ask airplane number three to twirl forward one time while the red airplane takes four steps on tiptoes.

Helicopters

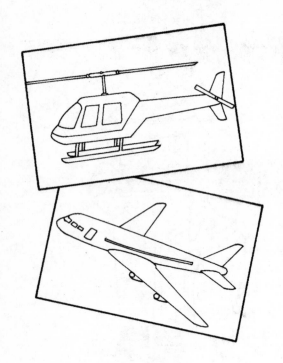

Helpful Helicopters

Your children probably know that helicopters carry people and things from one place to another just like airplanes. But they also have many unexpected uses. Because they can land almost anywhere, they can be used to take people to hospitals, or to deliver mail, food, or other supplies to hard-to-reach places. Because they can *hover* (stay still in the sky), helicopters can be used to lift heavy equipment or search for and rescue lost people. News teams fly helicopters over roads and highways and report how busy they are. Farmers use helicopters to spray chemicals on their fields to keep bugs away or make plants grow.

Bring in pictures or models of helicopters and airplanes for your group. Help the children compare the likes and differences.

Spiral Art

Give each of your children a paper plate. Let them paint their paper plates any colors they wish. When the plates have dried, help the children use scissors to cut around and around in a spiral shape. Staple a small piece of yarn to one end. Display your group's spirals by hanging them from the ceiling by the yarn. Encourage the children to watch them spin around like a propeller as they hang.

Helipads

Helicopters can land and take off in almost any open space large enough to fit them. These takeoff and landing sites are called *helipads*. Helipads can be found in the most unlikely places, such as on top of buildings, on mountain ledges, or in the middle of the jungle or desert.

Help your children create helipads around your room for their toy helicopters. Encourage them to make their helipads on a variety of surfaces at many different levels. For example, a helipad could be atop a block tower, on a shelf, on a chair, under a table, inside an empty container, or atop an overturned basket or box. If you wish, have the children use masking tape to mark off an X where the helicopter should land.

Vertical Lines

Gather your children around a blackboard or easel. Explain to them that a helicopter rises straight up in the air when it takes off, and can move straight down to land. Use chalk or markers to draw this up-and-down motion. Then tell the children that up-and-down lines are called *vertical lines*. Have the children take turns making vertical lines on the blackboard or easel.

Extension: Helicopters can also fly horizontally. Let the children practice making both up-and-down (vertical) and side-to-side (horizontal) lines.

Magnetic Landings

Collect various magnetic letters, including several upper and lowercase *H*s. Attach the magnets to a baking sheet, and scramble them all around. Explain to your children that *helicopter* begins with the letter *H*. Provide a small toy helicopter, and have the children locate and land on all of the *H*s. Scramble the magnets after each turn.

Variation: Cut large letters out of felt, fabric, or construction paper, and scatter them on the floor. Have the children pretend to be helicopters and land only on the letter *H*.

Rotor Stretch

A helicopter rotor is really a wing that spins around in a spiral to help push the helicopter skyward. Invite your children to pretend they are helicopter rotors. First have them spread out so that there is more than an arm's length between each child. Then instruct them to hold their arms out to their sides and to plant their feet firmly on the floor. Show them how to swivel their hips and arms first to one side, then to the other, keeping their feet still. Challenge the children to stretch as far as they can to both sides without moving their feet.

Once your children have mastered this stretch, let them move their feet and spin all the way around. Encourage them to spin slowly so they won't get too dizzy or bump into each other.

Hint: One way to control spinning is to have the children locate a landmark on a wall, such as a doorframe, a picture, or a window. With each turn, have the children find their landmark.

Turn of the Screw

A rotor turns on a helicopter the same way a belt is threaded through a nut or a screw turns in wood or metal. Drill several holes of several sizes in a small board. Provide the children with different sizes of screws that correspond to the holes. Have the children match each screw to its proper hole. Then help them use screwdrivers to screw them in.

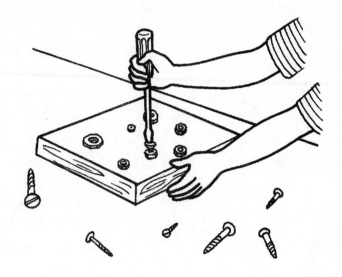

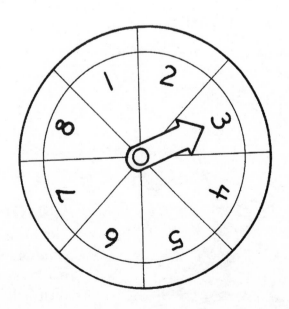

Number Spinner

Use a marker to divide a paper plate into four to 12 sections, depending on the ages and abilities of your children. Write a different number in each section. Cut an arrow shape out of cardboard or stiff paper, and attach it to the center of the plate with a metal paper fastener. Have one child at a time spin the arrow. What number does it point to? Or call out a number and have a child move the arrow to the correct section.

Variation: Instead of using a paper plate, modify an existing gameboard spinner for this activity.

Spinning Toys

Bring in a variety of spinning toys, such as tops, pinwheels, game spinners, jacks, dreidels, and record players. Invite your children to observe and play with them. Then have them look around your room for other things that spin, such as toy car wheels, the hands of a clock, and the blades of a fan.

Balloons & Blimps

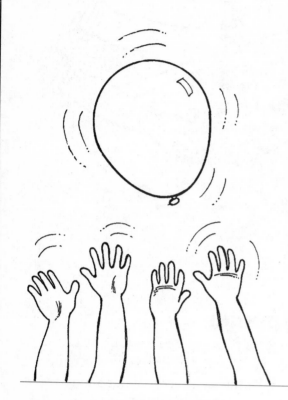

Balloon Toss

In ballooning you must travel where the wind takes you. A balloon pilot can control only how high a balloon flies and how smoothly it lands.

Have several of your children stand in a circle and pretend that they are air currents helping a hot air balloon move through the sky. Toss a balloon into the circle, and encourage the children to try to keep it up in the air using their hands. Sing the Floating Balloon song as you play.

Variation: On a late spring day, demonstrate what air currents are to your children by providing them with dandelions that have gone to seed. (Or have them pick their own if your play yard has them!) Have the children shake and blow the dandelions so that the seeds catch the wind and scatter in all directions.

Floating Balloon

Sung to: "Row, Row, Row Your Boat"

Float, float, float the balloon

Gently through the air.

Riding on a river of wind,

How'd it get up there?

Carol Gnojewski

Colorful Balloons

Hot air balloons are very colorful. Provide each of your children with a construction paper balloon shape. Set out markers, and let the children draw pictures or patterns on their balloons.

Layering

A balloon pilot steers a balloon by moving it up and down during flights to find the layer of air that is moving in the direction the balloon should go. Talk about layers with your children. Bring in items or pictures of items that have layers, such as layers of noodles in lasagna, layers of cotton in a quilt, layers of tissue in a facial tissue box, or layers of dirt and rocks in a terrarium.

Fill a clear-plastic container with layers of child-safe sensory materials such as cornmeal, dirt, pebbles, sand, or rice. Provide extra bowls of these materials plus empty clear-plastic containers near your sensory table. Encourage the children to use your layered container as a model for making layered containers of their own.

Extension: Help your children prepare a layered snack, such as layers of fruit and yogurt.

Balloon Chase

Groups of people (called chase crews) follow the flight of a balloon in a chase vehicle, such as a car or truck. Their job is to be at the landing site when the balloon touches down and to help pack up the balloon and return everyone to the launch site. The crew and the balloon pilot communicate with each other using walkie-talkies.

Divide your group into balloon pilots and chase crews for this version of Hide-and-Seek. The chase crew must cover their eyes while the balloon pilots hide a balloon or ball. Once the balloon is hidden, the chase crew searches for it. Encourage the balloon crew to help the chase crew find the balloon by telling the crew if they are near or far from the hiding place.

Variation: Play this game outside. Provide walkie-talkies for your children to communicate with.

Gas Balloon

In a gas balloon, the balloon is filled with a gas that is lighter than air, such as helium or hydrogen. Try the following science experiment with your children to give them a better understanding of how gas balloons work.

Place 1 cup of warm water in a glass soft-drink bottle. Add 2 tablespoons yeast and 1 tablespoon sugar. Cover the opening of the bottle and shake it vigorously. Then stretch a balloon over the mouth of the bottle. The yeast and sugar will react in the warm water to form carbon dioxide. Over a 1-hour period, the gas will fill up the bottle and move into the balloon, causing it to inflate.

Hint: Reinforce safety habits by wearing goggles during experiments such as this that involve chemical reactions.

Inflate–Deflate

Have your children help you blow up a beach ball using a small air pump. Point out how the deflated ball's shape is changed when it is inflated with air. Then let the children deflate the balloon by opening and squeezing the nozzle. Have the children listen and put their hands over the nozzle. What makes the hissing noise? What do they feel? Discuss other items, such as tires, air mattresses, and inner tubes, which can be inflated and deflated.

Balloon Basket

Balloonists ride in large baskets or *gondolas* attached to the balloon envelope. Bring in a large laundry basket to represent a balloon gondola. Encourage your children to use the basket for pretend balloon flight adventures. Where do they hope the balloon will take them? What do they see as they look down below?

Balloon Snack

Make popcorn in a hot air popper. Talk about how the air heats up the kernels to make them pop. This is similar to how heat affects the air to keep balloons afloat. Serve the snack in lined wicker baskets.

Balloon Stretch

Recite the following rhyme with your children for an "uplifting" circle time stretch.

Giant balloon floating away,
   (While seated, raise hands over your head in a circle shape.)

Where will the wind take us today?

Rise up, up, up—to the clouds we will touch.
   (Slowly stand up and reach for imaginary clouds.)

Drift down, down, down to land in the town.
   (Slowly sink to the floor.)

Carol Gnojewski

Blimps Have Rudders

Blimps are basically large gas balloons with engines that help move them through the air. Unlike balloons, their direction and speed is easily controlled. Airship pilots trap the wind in their rudders to help them steer.

To demonstrate how the wind can change the direction of an object, make a pinwheel for your class. Like a rudder, the vanes of a pinwheel trap the air to make them move. Cut a large square out of construction paper. Make four cuts in the square as shown in the illustration. Bring four of the corners (indicated by dots) to the center of the square. Hold the corners in place with a brass paper fastener. Slip the fastener through a small slit near the top of a straw.

Variation: Purchase pinwheels inexpensively from gardening, craft, or toy stores. Set them outside for your children to watch as they play.

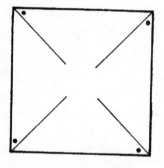 

Light and Heavy

A blimp is filled with gas that is lighter than air. With your children, talk about things that are light and things that are heavy. Fill a basket with heavy and light toys, and have your children compare them.

Extension: Bring in a helium-filled mylar balloon for your children to play with.

Hovering

Blimps are used by the military for surveillance work and by scientists as observation platforms. They are suited for these jobs because they can hover in one place for days at a time without making noise. On a hectic day, gather your children in a circle and talk about what it means to hover. Let them pretend that they are blimps hovering over land or water. Encourage the children to see how long they can stand or sit still quietly in one place.

Class Blimp

Most blimps are used as advertising gimmicks. They can vary in size and shape from the traditional Goodyear airship to the whimsical giant character floats flown in the annual Macy's Thanksgiving Parade.

Invite your children to make a blimp for your room. To make the blimp, have your children decorate the outside of a large white garbage bag. When they are finished decorating, show them how to stuff the bag with crumpled newspaper. Fasten the top with a twist tie. Hang the blimp from the ceiling near the door of your room, where visitors are sure to see it.

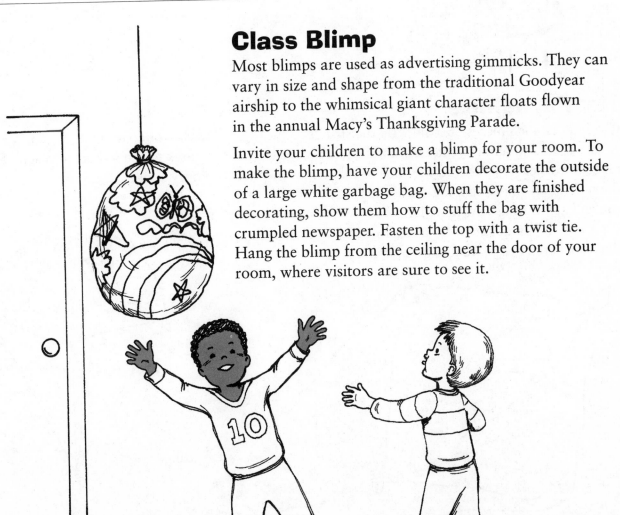

Parachutes

Parachute Drop

Parachutes help skydivers—people who have trained to jump out of airplanes—travel safely from the sky to the ground. Air gets trapped inside an open parachute, which allows the skydiver to fall slowly. Parachutes are also used to drop supplies, such as food, cars, animals, and other loads, to places that are hard to reach. Help your children make the Toy Parachute in the activity below. Simultaneously drop a spool and a Toy Parachute from a chair or stairwell. See if your children can predict which will drop faster and which will drop slower.

Toy Parachute

Cut four 12-inch pieces of string. Tie the strings to the corner of an old handkerchief or fabric square, one string on each corner. Then thread the ends of the strings through the hole in an empty spool. Tie the ends in a knot too big to slip back through the hole. Let your children take turns dropping the parachute from a chair or stairwell. See if they can catch the parachute in midair.

Variation: Tie small toys or action figures to the strings in place of the empty spool.

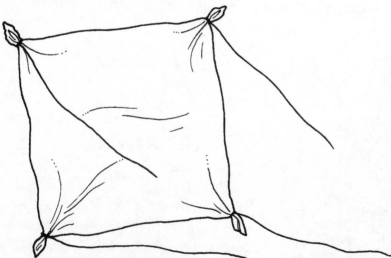

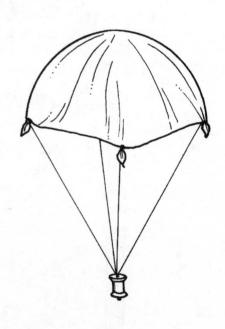

Strapped In

Skydivers wear a *harness*, a series of straps that support the body when the parachute is opened. Steering lines are attached to the harness. By pulling on the steering lines, jumpers can have more control over where they land and how fast they fall. Help your children experience what it's like to ride on a harness. Have one child at a time sit on a swing in your play yard. Invite each child to pretend that the swing is a harness and the ropes on the swing are attached to a big parachute canopy. Show the child how to move from side to side by pulling on the ropes.

Extension: Talk about how other vehicles are steered, such as cars, boats, horses, and trains.

Free Fall

Skydivers fall through the sky with their belly facing the ground. Have your children lie on the floor on their stomach. Can they lift their legs off the floor? Their arms? Demonstrate how to lift both legs and arms at once. Help the children lift both so that they can experience what this feels like. This is the position a skydiver uses to move around in the air during free fall, the period of time between jumping and pulling the ripcord to open the parachute.

Variation: Provide dollies or wagons for older children to scoot around in on their bellies. This is how some skydivers practice maneuvering toward each other for formations.

Geronimo!

In movies and cartoons, skydiving characters often yell "Geronimo!" as they jump, to signal to others that they're going down. When you yell "Geronimo," have your children scramble onto the floor in the free-fall position. Then yell "Ripcord!" That is their cue to pull on an imaginary string and stand up.

Variation: Encourage your children to think of a fun new word to use in place of *Geronimo.*

Skydiving Science

Parachutists try to land in a target area or spot. A large, bright-colored windsock often marks off this area. Before the first jump of the day, a skydiving pilot will drop nylon streamers out of the airplane to check wind conditions. By observing where the streamers land, the pilot can figure out where to fly the plane and when to tell the skydivers to jump so that they will land near the target.

On a windy day, drop paper or nylon fabric streamers from the top of a ladder or your playground equipment. Have your children use rocks, a flag, or another type of marker to mark the place where they land. Try this experiment again on the next windy day. Do the streamers fall in the same place?

Jump Zone

As they learn about skydiving, your children will want to practice jumping. To encourage safe play, designate one area in your room or your play yard as a jump zone. Cushion this area with blankets, hay, old mattresses, or large pillows for soft, injury-free landings. If you wish, provide children with skydiving safety gear, such as helmets, gloves, goggles, and backpack.

Pack on the Back

A skydiver wears a container that looks like a big backpack. It holds the main parachute, a reserve parachute, and the wires that attach the parachute to the skydiver's harness. Contact your local skydiving training center. Perhaps an instructor could visit your class and demonstrate how a parachute pack is prepared! Or ask if they could loan you some of their equipment. Being able to see and maybe even touch a real parachute would be a memorable experience.

Variation: Bring in several backpacks for your children to wear as they practice jumping in your jump zone. Stuff them with crumpled newspaper to add bulk without much weight.

Extension: Serve small boxes of raisins, granola bars, or other individually wrapped finger food out of a backpack during snacktime.

Parachute Placement

Explain to your children that some parachute canopies are round like an umbrella, and some are rectangular like the wings of an airplane. (Rectangular parachutes have a larger surface area, which produces a softer, more accurate landing.) Then cut several circles and rectangles out of felt for parachutes. Cut out an airplane shape as well. Arrange a piece of brown yarn across the middle of a flannelboard. The yarn line represents the ground. Place the airplane shape in the "sky" above the ground. Let your children arrange the parachute shapes on the flannelboard as you give them directions such as these that make use of the positional words they know: "Place two rectangular parachutes next to the airplane. Place a rectangular parachute on the ground line. Place one round parachute under the plane."

Variation: Have your children sort round and rectangle shapes.

Parachute Games

There are many no-lose cooperative games that you can play with your preschoolers using a nylon parachute. These can be purchased at many specialty toy stores and school supply stores. Or use a large piece of fabric, such as a king-size sheet. The games on page 173 will get you started.

Parachute Lift

Spread the parachute on the floor. Have your children stand in a circle around the parachute and grab onto it with both hands. Reinforce the opposites *up* and *down* as you have them slowly raise and lower the chute together. If you wish, place lightweight balls, such as whiffle balls, in the center of the parachute. Encourage your children to try to keep the balls from rolling off as they raise and lower the parachute.

Variation: Have the children flap the parachute up and down to make the whiffle balls pop into the air like popcorn.

The Sky Is Falling

Have your children hold onto the edges of the parachute and practice moving their arms up and down. Then have them raise their arms as high as they can and take a step forward. Show them how to lower their arms behind them as they lower their bodies, and sit down under the parachute. This will trap a pocket of air inside the parachute, creating a tentlike space for a short time. The children will have fun singing the following song as they watch the parachute "sky" slowly fall on their heads.

Henny Penny
Sung to: "Pop! Goes the Weasel"

Henny Penny sat under a tree

When down dropped an acorn.

It fell on her head, so poor Penny said,

"Look! The sky is falling."

Carol Gnojewski

Extension: Read to or tell your children the story of Henny Penny. Your local librarian should be able to direct you to one of the many delightful adaptations available in print.

Space Vehicles

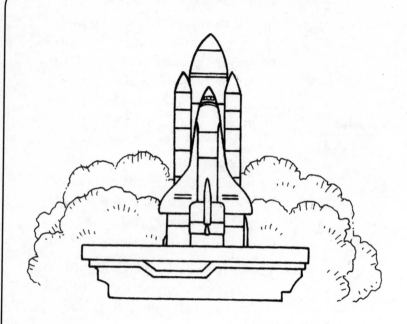

I'm a Space Shuttle

I'm a space shuttle

Ready for flight.

Climb onboard and hold on tight.

When it's time for liftoff into space,

Help me count, and up we'll race.

10, 9, 8, 7, 6, 5, 4, 3, 2, 1—Blastoff!

Diane Thom

Mini Space Shuttles

Collect a rectangular tissue box for each of your children. Then cut two large triangles for each child out of cardboard, posterboard, or stiff paper. Help the children glue the triangles to the bottom of their tissue boxes for orbiter wings. Give each child one-fourth of a paper towel tube to glue to the front of the box as shown in the illustration. Then have the children paint their orbiters with silver paint. You may decide to provide bits of foil, chenille strips, and other collage materials for the children to scatter over the wet silver paint.

Variation: Provide the children with pictures of spacecraft. Then set out various recyclable materials, including small boxes, potato crisp cans, egg cartons, and plastic containers. Invite the children to use these materials to construct their own spacecraft.

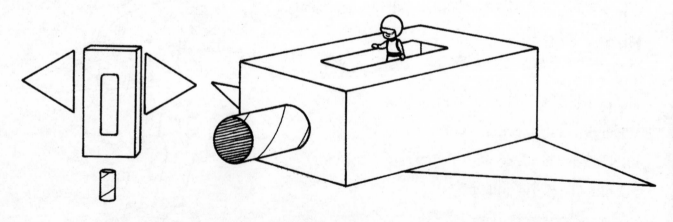

Shuttle Countdown

Teach your children to count backward for a space shuttle countdown! Cut a rocket shape for each of them out of different colors of construction paper (or duplicate the rocket pattern on page 179). Number the shapes with numerals from 1 to 10. As you count down, encourage the children to hold up their rockets as the numbers are called. At the end of the countdown, shout "Blastoff!" and have the children launch their rocket shapes around the room.

Space Shuttles

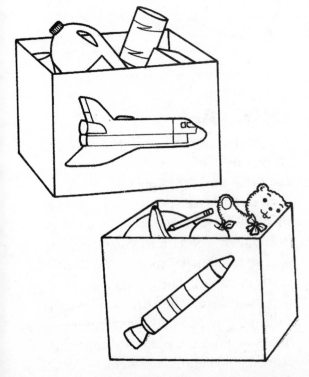

Explain to your children that a space shuttle is a vehicle used to transport people and equipment into outer space. When space shuttles are launched, special rockets called rocket boosters blast the spacecraft straight up in the air like a firework. The rocket boosters aren't reusable. Once the space shuttle is high enough, they drop into the ocean with the help of parachutes. The part of the space shuttle that remains is the *orbiter*, which looks like a stubby airplane. It can be used over and over again. At the end of a space mission, the orbiter glides down to the ground and lands on a runway just like an airplane.

Find two boxes. Place a picture or sticker of a space shuttle on one box, and a picture or sticker of a rocket on the other box. Then collect a variety of toys, food, and other materials. Help your children put the reusable or recyclable items into the space shuttle box and the non-recyclable materials into the rocket box.

Spacecraft Fingerplay

Use the patterns on page 179 to make flannelboard figures for the following fun fingerplay!

Five Shiny Spacecraft

One shiny spacecraft flying to the moon,

Along comes another. Then there are two.

Two shiny spacecraft speed through the galaxy.

Another blasts off. Then there are three.

Three shiny spacecraft ready to explore.

Along comes another. Now there are four.

Four shiny spacecraft soar and dive.

Along comes another. Now there are five.

Five shiny spacecraft are coming home soon.

What an adventure they had on the moon!

Diane Thom

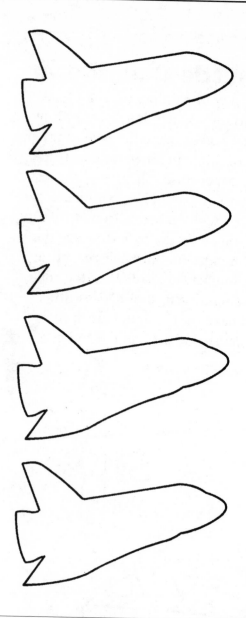

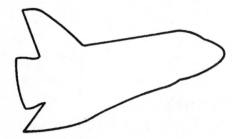

Orbit Art

Let your children use markers to color sheets of white dot stickers as the earth and other planets. Have each child place several stickers on a sheet of dark blue or black construction paper. Explain to your children that space shuttles move around the earth in circles. The circular paths they make are called *orbits*. Have the children practice making circular orbits around the planets using white crayons or metallic markers.

Zero-Gravity Floaters

Explain to your children that in space there is no up or down. People and objects don't weigh as much as they do on earth, so they will float away if they aren't held down with rope, Velcro, belts, or magnets. For example, if you wanted to drink a cup of juice, the juice would not fall into your mouth or stay in your cup. Instead, it would float out of the cup and around the room in big juice drops!

Gather your children in a circle and invite them to make believe they are astronauts in space. Then use a bubble wand to blow bubbles around the room. Have the children pretend that the bubbles are food, utensils, tools, or other items you might need to live and work on a spacecraft. Encourage them to try to catch the bubbles before they pop or float out of their reach.

Space Food

Most food in space needs to be dried so that it won't spoil or take up storage room. Astronauts mix the dried food with water and heat it in microwave ovens. Provide your children with dried, flaked, or powdered foods, such as dried fruit, sun-dried tomatoes, bean flakes, potato flakes, dried soup mix, or powdered eggs. Let the children experiment with using water to reconstitute these foods. Do these foods look and taste different when they are fresh?

Variation: Bring in packages of freeze-dried food for the children to explore. These can be found at some sporting goods stores or sports outfitters.

Shuttle Snack

Give each of your children a pineapple ring for a launch pad. Have them place one half of a peeled banana upright inside the ring for the shuttle orbiter. If you wish, squirt non-dairy whipped topping around the pineapple for the propulsion smoke. Your children will enjoy launching their shuttles into their mouth!

Astronaut Dress-up

Help your children develop space suits and equipment for outer space play. Provide the children with foil, packing peanuts, plastic tubing, phone cords, plastic foam, and other miscellaneous materials to decorate these items. Here are just a few ideas:

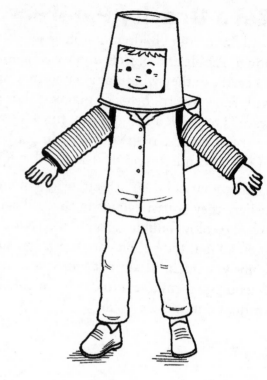

- **Portable Life-support Backpack**—Cut four vertical slits on one side of an empty detergent box as shown in the illustration. Thread heavy ribbon through the slits and tie the ends together to make two loops large enough for your children's arms. Let the children paint and decorate the box.

- **Bubble Helmet**—Turn a clean food bucket, such as a movie popcorn bucket, upside down. Cut a large square hole on one side. Then cut a piece of light-colored cellophane larger than the square. Cover the square hole with the cellophane square and use tape to attach it to the inside of the bucket. (You might ask local fast-food chains or movie theatres to donate their food or snack buckets.)

- **Shuttle Control Booth**—Let your children use metallic paint to paint the inside and outside of a sturdy cardboard box. When the paint is dry, have the children glue buttons and controls to the inside of the box flaps to make control panels. Dot stickers, file labels, buttons, drawer knobs, washers, square or hexagon nuts, and paper clips are just a few of the materials your children could use to complete their panels.

- **Robot Arms**—Purchase vinyl duct (available inexpensively at hardware and home improvement stores). Cut the duct into two foot sections. Slip each section over the armholes of a long-sleeve oversize shirt. Use strong duct tape to tape the duct to the sleeves. To wear, have the children place their arms through the shirtsleeves.

Space Flannelboard Figures

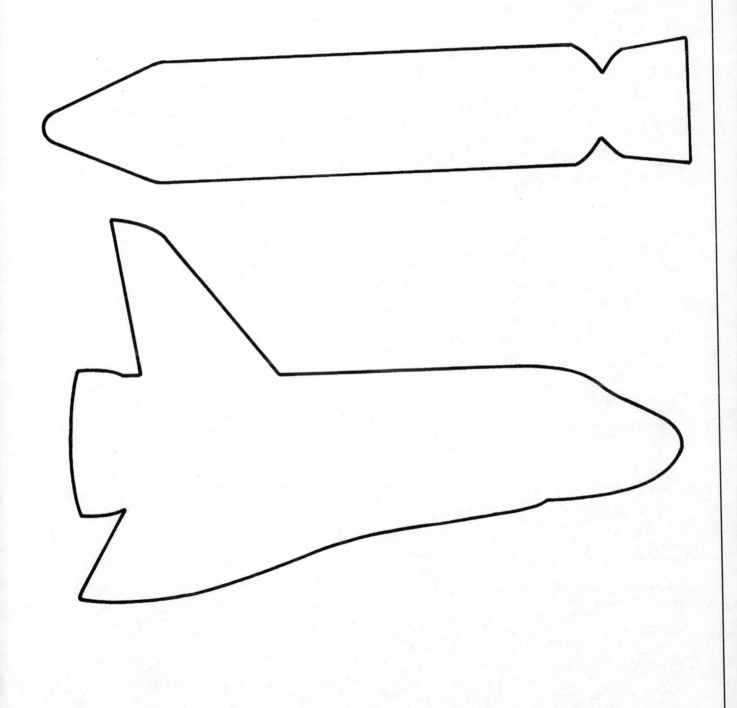

On the Water

Canals

Gutter Canal

Explain to your children that canals are small waterways that flow into lakes and oceans. Boats travel on canals to get to and from the larger bodies of water. Canals are man-made. They have to be dug out of the ground with power tools and construction vehicles.

Have your children use sand tools to dig a long, narrow hole in your sand table or box. Help them set a plastic gutter (available inexpensively and in varying lengths at your local hardware or building supply store) in the hole. As a group, pack sand under and around the gutter to level and stabilize it. Fill the gutter with water. Let the children use their Gutter Canal for play with toy boats and other waterproof toys.

Loaf Locks

Canals are sometimes built in sections. Each section is called a lock. Make a canal lock using two identical loaf pans. Line up the loaf pans in a tub or wading pool so that the handle of the first pan rests on top of the handle of the second pan. Slightly elevate the other side of the first pan by wedging a small block underneath it. Fill both pans half full with water.

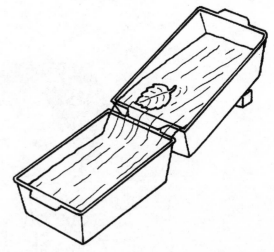

Provide your children with leaves, craft sticks, small Lego blocks, or other lightweight items that float. Let the children place these items in the first pan. Then have the children slowly add more water to the first pan. Can they predict what will happen? Have the children raise the water level in the first pan until their items float over the handles and into the second pan. This is similar to the way that the level of water in canal locks is raised or lowered to allow boats and barges to travel from higher to lower levels and vice versa.

Canal Path Math

Use blue chalk to draw two lake shapes on a chalkboard not more than 12 inches apart. Invite one of your children at a time to use the blue chalk to make a canal (a line) connecting the two lakes. If you wish, help the children use a ruler to make their canal lines straight.

Variation: Place two carpet squares apart from each other in your room. Tell the children they are two lakes. Have the children pretend that craft sticks or Lincoln Logs are the locks (sections) of a canal. Invite them to use the craft sticks or Lincoln Logs to make a canal between the two lakes. Then have them count how many "locks" they used to make their canal.

Deep and Shallow Water

Canals are dug either very deep, so that big ships can pass through them, or shallow, for flat-bottomed boats such as rafts and barges. Help your children understand the concepts *deep* and *shallow*. Bring in two same-size cups. Fill one cup with water to the top, and add just a little water to the other. Explain that the water in the first cup is *deep* because there is a lot of it. The water in the second cup is *shallow* because there isn't much of it. Set out a variety of same-size containers. First, have the children fill the containers so that the water in them is deep. Then have them fill the containers so that the water in them is shallow.

Variation: Do this activity with containers of various sizes. How does the size of the container affect what is deep and what is shallow?

Extension: Ask older preschoolers why big ships need deep water and barges don't. What might happen if a big ship entered a shallow canal?

Tugboat Pull

During movement time, have your children pair off. Encourage one child to pretend to be the tugboat while the other pretends to be a barge. Have the tugboat gently push or pull the barge around the room in a box or wagon. Let the pairs change places so that each gets to be both a tugboat and a barge.

Variation: Attach wagons or boxes to riding toys and play this game in your play yard.

Tugboat Song

I'm a little tugboat, strong and small.

I pull barges down a canal.

I will tug and chug the whole way through

To bring cars and food just for you.

Substitute the names of other products loaded on barges in place of *cars* and *food*.

Carol Gnojewski

Craft Stick Barge

Tape or glue five craft sticks together side by side. Let your children float the barge in the water table. Let them place a toy car on top of the barge and float it from one end to the table to another. Will the barge hold more than one car?

Snack Barges

Give each of your children a spoon and a small bowl filled with milk. Set out trays of square- or rectangular-shaped cereal, such as Shredded Wheat or Chex brand cereals. Have your children pretend that the cereal pieces are rafts or barges. Let them float the cereal in their bowls. They will enjoy using their spoons to tow the "barges" into their mouth.

Canoes & Rowboats

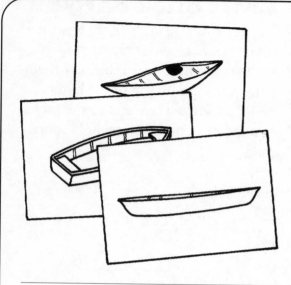

Boat Stories

Show your children pictures of small, hand-powered boats including canoes, kayaks, and rowboats. Ask your children if they have ever ridden in one of these boats. Invite them to talk about their experiences. Who did they go with? Where did they go? Who paddled the boat?

Extension: Have the children tell you about a boat trip that they would like to take. If you wish, write the boat stories your children dictate on a bulletin board for the parents to read.

Oar Discovery

Canoes, kayaks, and rowboats are rowed and steered by hand using oars. The type of oar varies for each boat. If possible, bring in real oars for your children to explore. Point out their similarities and differences. Canoe oars have a handle and a single blade. Kayak oars have two blades: one for each end. Rowboat oars have pins that lock onto the boat to keep them secure.

Extension: While you are studying boats, keep a set of small oars in your dress-up area, along with life jackets, binoculars, fishing gear, and tackle boxes.

Different Strokes

Place a small wading pool in the middle of your play area. Have your children pretend that the pool is a canoe or kayak. Provide empty gift-wrap or paper towel tubes for oars (or use real plastic oars). Kneeling in the "boat," demonstrate for the children the different paddling techniques required for each boat.

Canoe— Hold the oar with one hand at the top and one hand near the blade. Steer the canoe by paddling first on one side and then on the other. (If two people are in the canoe, have each child paddle different sides.)

Kayak— Hold the oar in its center and gently dip one blade into the water on one side of the boat and the other blade into the water on the other side of the boat.

Rowboat Play

Bring a real rowboat and put it in your play yard. Let your children use it as a play structure. Encourage children to take short pretend boat trips. (Be sure to supervise if you choose to provide oars.)

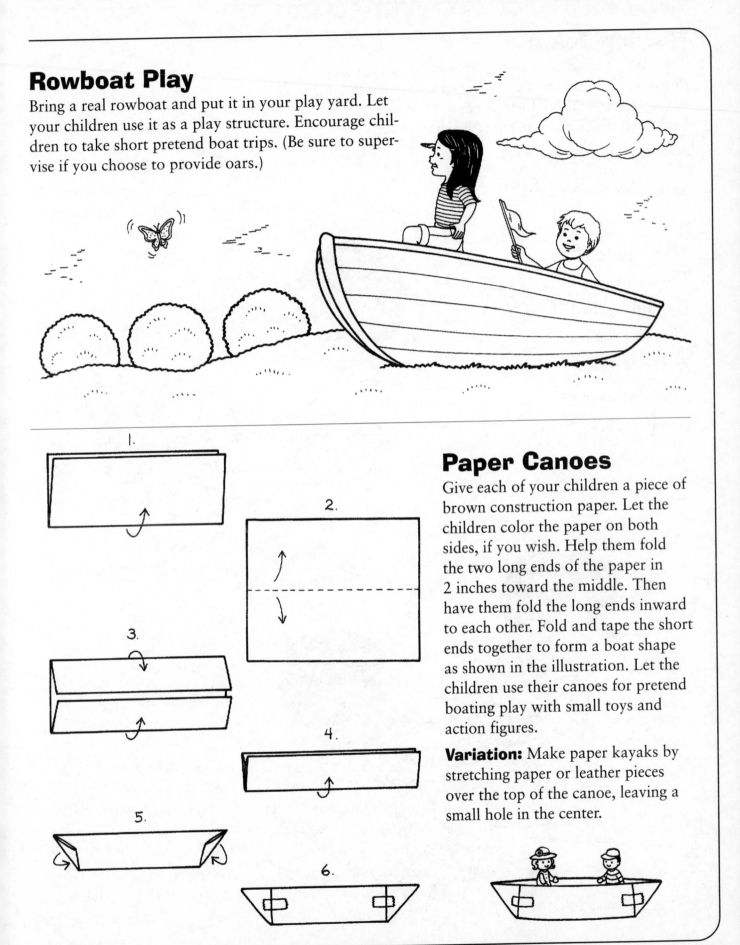

Paper Canoes

Give each of your children a piece of brown construction paper. Let the children color the paper on both sides, if you wish. Help them fold the two long ends of the paper in 2 inches toward the middle. Then have them fold the long ends inward to each other. Fold and tape the short ends together to form a boat shape as shown in the illustration. Let the children use their canoes for pretend boating play with small toys and action figures.

Variation: Make paper kayaks by stretching paper or leather pieces over the top of the canoe, leaving a small hole in the center.

Rowing Team

Ask your children to sit on the floor in pairs. As they sit down, have each pair of children face one another, hold hands, and touch feet. Invite them to rock forward and backward gently while singing "Rowing Team."

Sung to: "Rock-A-Bye Baby"

Move your hands forward

As far as they'll go,

Then pull them back—

That's how you row!

Forward and back,

We'll row as a team,

And cross the lake

As smooth as cream.

Carol Gnojewski

Canoe Snacks

The first canoes were made by digging out logs. Your children will have fun using spoons and melon ballers to dig out the pulp of fruits and vegetables to make canoe-like snacks. The following are suggestions for making and filling edible snack boats.

Fruit Canoes

Cantaloupe—Slice in half, scoop out the fruit with a melon baller, and fill the halves with a mixture of grapes and cantaloupe balls.

Banana—Slice the banana peel across the top. Scoop out the fruit and fill the peel with marshmallows, chocolate chips, and chunks of banana. Microwave to melt the marshmallows and chips, if desired.

Orange—Slice in half, scoop out the fruit, and fill the halves with a mixture of orange pulp and fruit cocktail.

Kiwi—Slice in half, scoop out the fruit, and fill with strawberries and kiwi chunks.

Watermelon—Slice in half, scoop out the fruit with a melon baller, and fill with the watermelon balls.

Vegetable Canoes

Zucchini—Slice zucchini lengthwise and scoop out the soft inner part. Fill the halves with chunks of zucchini mixed with creamed corn. If you wish, boil the zucchini halves till tender before filling.

Celery—Chop celery into 3- to 4-inch sections. Fill with cream cheese or peanut butter.

Tomato—Remove tops. Scoop out the fruit and fill with a mixture of tomato chunks, soft bread crumbs, and grated cheese.

Eggplant—Slice in half lengthwise. Scoop out the pulp and fill with chunks of cooked eggplant mixed with salsa or humus.

Ferries

Island Hopping

Explain to your children that ferries are part of a highway system on the water. They carry people and vehicles to and from islands. Have any of your children been on a ferryboat or visited an island?

Bring in books or magazines with pictures and information about both ferries and islands. Then help your children create an island in your water table. Encourage them to experiment with a variety of island-building materials, such as rocks, fish tank gravel (available at most pet stores), wooden blocks, sand, sticks, and clay. Let the children use small toy boats to ferry action figures to their island.

Variation: With your children, build an island area out of carpet squares, blocks, or other materials. Place it in the middle of your floor "ocean." Designate another area as the "mainland." Let the children use toy boats or wagons to ferry themselves back and forth between the two areas.

Island Snack

At snacktime, serve a cocktail of fruits that are grown in various island climates, such as bananas, coconuts, pineapples, mangoes, papayas, and fresh berries.

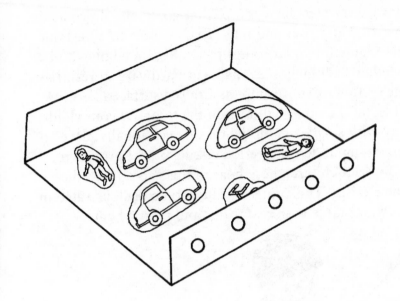

Group Ferryboat

Make a ferryboat out of posterboard or stiff construction paper. Fold the short edges in 2 inches. Then have your children put dot stickers on the outside of one folded edge for port-holes. Provide the children with car magazines, and have them tear or cut out pictures of cars and trucks. Help them glue the pictures in the middle of the ferryboat.

Variation: Use magazine pictures with stickers of vehicles.

Ferry Whistle

Explain to your children that ferryboat captains blow a whistle when the ferry leaves and enters a harbor. This is a signal to the ferry crews to do the work they need to do so the boat can leave or arrive safely. Bring in a whistle, and together with the children, develop whistle signals that mean different things throughout your day. For example, you might blow a whistle signal before each new activity.

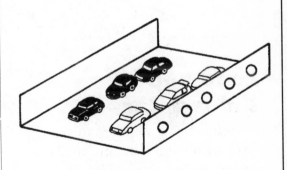

Ferry Sort

Fill your Group Ferryboat with a collection of small toy cars, such as Hot Wheels or Matchbox cars, of various sizes and colors. Have your children sort the cars into rows by color, size, or number.

Ramps

Many ferry piers have ramps that go up and down as the level of water rises and falls. To construct an adjustable ramp, attach two large 4x4 pieces of sanded plywood together with hinges (available at hardware stores). Lay one section of your ramp on a raised surface like a low table, let the other half rest on the floor. As your children play with small cars on the ramp, occasionally place something under the section resting on the ground to show your children how boat ramps can raise as the water raises. This principle can also be demonstrated in the water table with real water and plastic boats.

Load and Unload Cars

Encourage your children to set up a ferry terminal filled with small cars and trucks waiting to board the ferryboat. Then design a ramp and a large flatboat out of play construction materials such as blocks, building logs, or craft sticks. Show the children how to load the cars across or down your ramp. As the children play, suggest they load the ferryboat first single file (one car at a time). The next time, have them load the boat two cars at a time.

Ferryboat Game

Gather your children in a circle and take several giant steps backward. Invite the children to pretend that the center of the circle is an ocean. Then select one of the children to be the Ferryboat. Ask one child at a time to be the Ferryboat Rider, and to name a person in the circle he or she would like to travel through the "ocean" to visit. Sing the Ferryboat song below, and complete the third line with the name of the Ferryboat Rider. For example, if the Ferryboat Rider is named Trevor, then the child he has chosen to visit would sing, "Will you carry Trevor across the water to me?" The Ferryboat would then take the hand of the Ferryboat Rider and guide him or her through the ocean to his chosen destination. The Ferryboat Rider then takes a place in the circle next to his friend. Let the children take turns being the Ferryboat. Encourage the Ferryboat to blow a ferry whistle when the Ferryboat Rider has reached his or her destination, and to have fun finding a new route through the water to each person. Continue while interest lasts.

Variation: Play this game outside, using a wagon as the ferry.

Hint: This is a good game to play near the beginning of the year, to learn everyone's name.

Ferryboat Song
Sung to: "Pop! Goes the Weasel"

Ferry, ferry, ferryboat,

Floating on the sea,

Will you carry Trevor

Across the water to me?

Replace the name *Trevor* with the names of children in your group.

Carol Gnojewski

Harbors & Piers

Safe Harbor

Piers, which are platforms extending from the shore, are used as landing places for boats. Piers are found in areas of calm waters. We call these calm areas near the shoreline *harbors* because they are safe, protected places.

Talk with your children about places where they feel safe, such as at home, at school, or in a familiar neighborhood. Why do they feel safe and protected there? If you wish, explore ways to feel safe in your facility.

Pulleys

One of the main activities that occur in harbors is the loading and unloading of ships. Heavy cargo is often transferred from boats to piers using large cranes or pulley systems.

Help your children construct a pulley in your room by attaching a pulley securely to a wood ceiling joist in your room. (Small pulleys and thin rope are available at hardware stores.) String a rope through the pulley. Then tie a small basket to one end of the rope. Encourage your children to fill the basket with toys and then raise the basket by pulling down the other end of the rope.

Hint: You might decide you want a pulley as a permanent addition to your block area.

Let's Build a Pier

Place small boats and pictures of harbors and piers in your block area. Encourage your children to use the blocks to build piers for their boats.

Ask your children if they would like to build a large pier. This can be done indoors or outside, depending on the size of the pier and the materials used. Ask for parent help if this activity evolves into a large project.

Once construction is complete, develop rules for controlling the safe use of your pier. You may need to limit when the children can play on the pier and how many children can use it at one time. At right are a few ideas for extending play on your pier.

Fishing Pier—Transform your classroom pier into a fishing pier. Provide the children with small fishing poles, tackle boxes, and fishnets. Tie a small magnet to the end of each line and let your children catch paper fish with paper clips attached. Serve a snack of fish crackers, and encourage the children to count them as they eat.

Ferry Pier—Turn your pier into a ferry terminal. Build a ramp to accommodate toy cars, wagons, or trikes.

Swimming Pier—Let your children jump off the ramp and pretend to swim around the room. Bring in beach towels, rubber rafts, and diving gear to extend swimming play.

Entertainment Pier—Have your children take turns as performers and audience members as your group uses the pier for an entertainment stage. Tickets, microphones, and musical instruments are just a few props that would enhance this play experience.

Water Table Piers

Provide miscellaneous materials near the water table for your children to use to create boat piers, such as small landscape bricks, safe wooden blocks, and plastic planter boxes (use upside down). Tie small lengths of string to plastic boats. If possible, attach suction cup hooks to the sides of the piers from which the children can moor their boats.

Extension: As your children are playing in the water table with their piers and boats, have them practice their math skills. How many boats are in the harbor? How many boats are tied up at the pier?

Cork Buoys

Buoys are floating objects anchored near the entrance to a harbor to help guide ships safely to port. The shapes, colors, numbers, and markings of buoys tell a story about the water nearby.

Collect several corks to use as buoys and paint them different waterproof colors. Let your children decide what each buoy color stands for. For instance, a red cork buoy might mean that rocks are nearby. A yellow cork buoy might mean that the water level is low. A green one might mean that the water is deep.

Let your children use the Cork Buoys as they play with boats at your water table.

Cargo Cleanup

Bring in medium-sized boxes for your children to use as boats. First have them load their boats with "cargo" such as books, blocks, pillows, or dolls. Let them chug around the room pushing and pulling their cargo. Finally, have them return the cargo where it belongs. This is a clever way to interest the children in cleanup time!

Out in the Harbor

Sung to: "Down by the Station"

Out in the harbor
Early in the morning,
See the great big boats
Coming to unload.
See the little tugboat
Guiding in the freighter.
Huff, huff, puff, puff,
Off he goes!

Out in the harbor
Early in the morning,
See the great big boats
Tied up at the piers.
See the busy workers
Hauling off the cargo.
Huff, huff, puff, puff,
Off they go.

Jean Warren

Harbor Play Cloth

Create a tabletop Harbor Play Cloth for your children with a large piece of vinyl and some permanent marking pens. Mark off the shoreline and several piers. Draw waves to indicate water. Then give your children some toy boats and small items to load and unload onto the piers.

Harbor Mural

Cover a wall in your room with blue tissue paper. Make sure the area that you cover is at a height that your preschoolers can reach. Use the patterns on page 199 to make several photocopies of boats. Cut out the boat shapes and let each child paint or decorate a boat with crayons or markers. Label each boat with USS and the child's name, such as USS Tommy. Have each child use tape to attach his or her boat to the mural. Cut out brown construction paper pilings and piers and have the children arrange them on the paper to complete the harbor scene.

Harbor Patterns

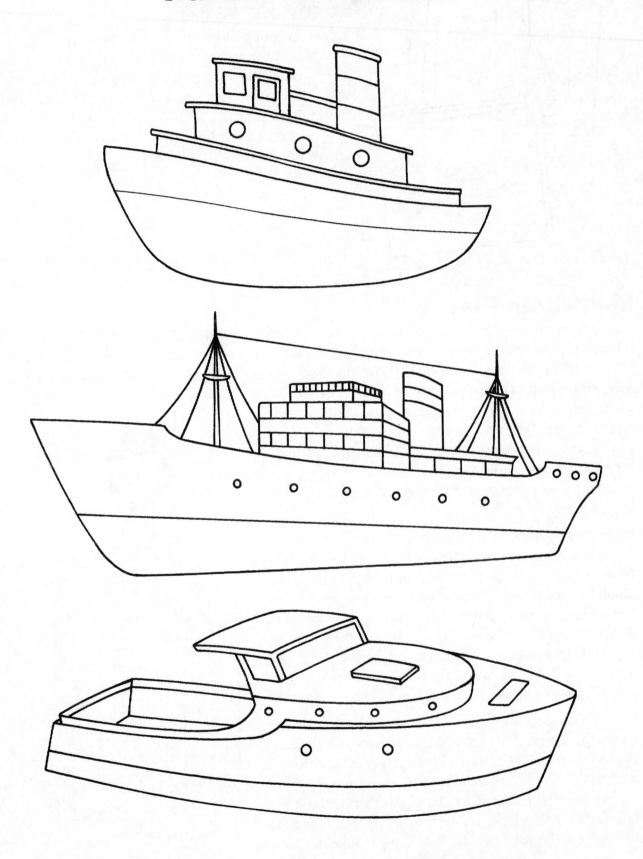

Motorboats

Motor Power

Explain to your children that motorboats are like racecars because they have motors that help move them through the water very quickly. Bring in pictures of a variety of different boats and other vehicles. Talk about what makes each vehicle go. Help the children sort the pictures into two piles: vehicles that have motors or engines, and vehicles that do not.

Motorboat Play

Motorboats can have *inboard* motors or *outboard* motors. Inboard motors are found inside the boat. You can start an inboard motor by turning a key, as you would to start a car. Motorboats with inboard motors are steered from the front of the boat using a steering wheel or *helm*. Outboard motors are found hanging outside the back of the boat. You can start most outboard motors by pulling on a starting rope, as you would to start a lawnmower. Motorboats with outboard motors are steered from the back of the boat using a handle or *tiller*.

Make a motorboat for your children to use in pretend motorboat play. Find an appliance box large enough for one or two of your children to sit in comfortably. Fold in or cut off all but one of the box flaps. Use a brad or small belt and nut to attach a sturdy paper-plate steering wheel or *helm* to the remaining flap. Then cut a small hole in the flap near the helm. Thread a piece of yarn through the hole and knot it to secure. Tie a real or toy key to the other end of the yarn. The side with the helm and key will be the front of the boat.

Down the center of the box, on the opposite side of the boat, cut a 6-inch vertical slit. Cut a large *L* shape from a discarded box flap to make a tiller. Then cut a small hole on one side of the tiller. Thread a piece of string through the hole for a starting rope, and tie it to secure. Slide the tiller through the slit, long arm down as shown in the illustration.

Extension: Look at pictures of motorboats and have your children try to decide if they have inboard or outboard motors.

Speed Crafts

Make the following motorboats with your children. If you wish, use them for motorboat play or racing in your water table or wading pool. Supervise children carefully around soap and balloons.

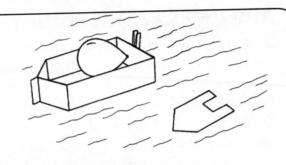

Balloon-Powered Motorboat

Cut a clean half-gallon cardboard milk carton in half lengthwise and discard one half. Poke a hole in the middle of what used to be the bottom of the carton. Pull a balloon through the hole so that the end of the balloon is hanging outside the carton (see illustration). Have the children watch as you blow up the balloon. Do not tie the end, but use a spring-type clothespin to secure it. Place the boat in a water table or wading pool and release the clothespin. The boat will race across the water.

Variation: Make two motorboats and let the children take turns racing them.

Soap-Powered Motorboat

To make this boat, cut a house shape out of a plastic foam food tray. Then cut a door shape out of the bottom of the house shape to complete the boat. Place the boat in a pan of water. Carefully put a few drops of liquid soap in the door-shaped opening of the boat, and let your children watch the boat move across the water. Try sprinkling salt or baking soda in the opening of the boat, or dropping oil or vinegar instead of soap. Do these materials make the boat go?

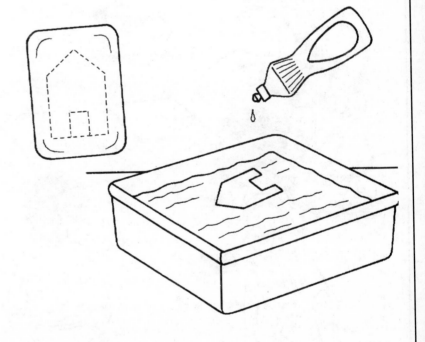

Motorboat Movement

Invite your children to sit in a circle, leaving a wide opening at one section of the circle. Place two carpet squares in the center of the circle. Choose two children to be motorboat drivers while the rest of the children recite the following Motorboat Chant. Have the children who are driving the motorboats start their motors. Then encourage them to first walk around the circle and then run as indicated in the chant. On the last line of the chant, have the children pretend to move their throttles forward to speed up their motors. Encourage the rest of the children to make motorboat noises. Let the motorboat drivers run faster and faster around the circle before shutting off their motors and coasting to the center to sit on the carpet squares. Repeat until every child has had an opportunity to run around the circle.

Motorboat Chant

Motorboat, motorboat,

Go so slow.

Motorboat, motorboat,

Go so fast.

Motorboat, motorboat,

Give it more gas—*vrrrm*!

Polly R. Reedy

Water Ski Discovery

Explain to your children that in the sport of water-skiing, people on special skis are pulled or *towed* across the top of the water by motorboats. Water-skiers hold onto ropes attached to the back of the motorboat, and as the boat moves, the skiers are pulled along behind it. If possible, bring in examples of waterskiing equipment for your children to explore. This might include tow ropes, skis, wet suits, buoy belts, life jackets, and kneeboards. Let your children experience trying on this equipment.

Extension: Bring in a video showing people water-skiing for fun or competition. These are available at your local library or video store.

Motorboat Snack

Serve your children their snacks in toy motorboats (or use permanent markers to draw motorboat shapes on paper plates). Fill each toy boat with fingerfoods such as raisins, small crackers, carrot slices, apple slices, and small pieces of cheese.

Ocean Liners

Our Ocean Liner

Explain to your children that ocean liners are big ships that carry people across oceans and seas. Help them discover what an ocean liner or cruise ship is like by sharing related books and pictures. Talk about your own experiences on a ship, and encourage the children to relate any experiences they may have had.

Invite them to help you set up an ocean liner or cruise ship in the home-life area. Help the children make a list of the equipment they want their cruise ship to have. Guide their thinking by asking them questions. How many decks and cabins should it have? Will it have a swimming pool, dining room, gym, or library? Will there be any entertainment? How many crew members will you need? Encourage them to come up with questions of their own. Together, think of ways to find out the answers. Perhaps you will need to invite a cruise director or travel agent to talk to the children and explain what they do. Help the children come up with ideas for making or collecting the items that they will need to complete their cruise ship.

Globe Trotters

Bring in a world map or globe. Point out all of the oceans and seas. Have any of your children seen an ocean? Help them decide which ocean they would like to cross on their pretend cruise.

Porthole Shapes

Explain to your children that most ships have portholes instead of windows. Portholes are round sealed windows that allow light to come into the cabin. Cut a circle out of the middle of a large piece of blue tissue paper and use it to cover one of the windows in your room. Your children will enjoy looking out the "porthole" to see what's happening outside.

Parts of a Boat

Sung to: "If You're Happy and You Know It"

There are four main parts of a boat.
  (Hold up four fingers.)

There are four main parts of a boat,

Four places you can go on any boat you know;

There are four main parts of a boat.

The bow is the front of the boat.
  (Walk forward.)

The bow is the front of the boat.

If you go near, you can watch the captain steer.
  (Pretend to steer the boat.)

The bow is the front of the boat.

The stern is the back of the boat.
  (Walk backward.)

The stern is the back of the boat.

If you walk back again to the ship's other end,

You'll see the stern is the back of the boat.

The starboard and the port are the sides.
  (Point one arm to the right and the other arm to the left.)

The starboard and the port are the sides.

On an ocean or a sea, in any country,

The starboard and the port are the sides.

Carol Gnojewski

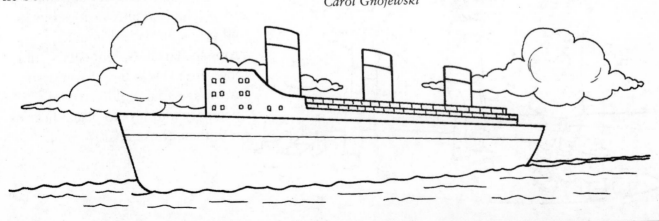

Anchors Aweigh!

Help your children cut or tear tissue paper or construction paper into thin strips to make confetti. Hand out paper sacks for each child to put their confetti into. Later, gather your children together in a circle. Choose one child to be the captain and have him or her stand in the middle of the circle. Instruct the captain to give the order "Anchors aweigh!" This is a signal for everyone to throw a handful of the confetti at the captain. Let the children take turns being the captain. Continue until you run out of confetti.

Hint: At the end of this activity, give the children brooms and dustpans. Have them pretend they are deckhands as they swab (clean up) the deck (floor).

Cruise Boat

Turn your block area into a cruise ship. Use masking tape to make a cruise boat outline on the floor. Make the boat shape large enough to hold several children plus various blocks and props. Provide dramatic play props such as hats, binoculars, and long cardboard tubes, if you wish. Encourage your children to take imaginary journeys to places near or far in their cruise boat.

Ocean Liner Dining

Food is plentiful on most cruise ships. In addition to dining rooms, lounges, and restaurants, each deck may have a buffet table stocked with food all day long. Turn your snack table into a buffet table. Cover it with a festive tablecloth. If you wish, purchase a paper centerpiece, or make your own centerpiece by adding flowers to a plastic vase or filling a large toy boat with real or plastic fruit. Keep nonperishable snacks on the table for your children to nibble on whenever they are hungry.

Deck Chairs

Bring in lawn chairs to use as pretend deck chairs. Add the chairs to your quiet area. Encourage your children to pretend they are on the deck of a ship as they stretch out on the chairs to relax or look at a book.

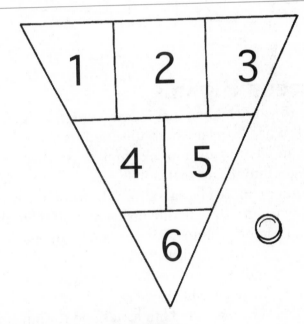

Numeral Shuffle

Shuffleboard is a game that is commonly played onboard the deck of a ship. Use chalk to draw a large inverted triangle on a floor or sidewalk. Divide the triangle into sections as shown in the illustration. Number the sections from 1 to 6, with the 6 at the tip and the 1 at the base of the triangle. Then let your children use a small push broom to push (or shuffle) jar lids toward the triangle. Invite them to continue "shuffling" until they land on the triangle. Have each child identify the number his or her lid lands on.

Rescue Boats

Rescue Boats

Show your children pictures of various rescue boats, such as Coast Guard cutters, fireboats, or police boats. Explain that these boats and the people on them help boaters who are in danger because of storms or perhaps their boats have broken down. After your discussion, sing the song at right.

Sung to: "Three Blind Mice"

Rescue boats,

Rescue boats.

Coast Guard cutters,

Fireboats.

If there's a fire or emergency

On an ocean or lake or on the sea,

The rescue boats will come for me.

Rescue boats.

Anonymous

Distress Signals

Explain to your children that a distress signal is a signal for help. When boats are in trouble, sailors shoot flares into the air. Flares look a lot like fireworks. They send a bright light into the air that can be seen on land. Have each of your children bring a flashlight from home. Show them how to turn their flashlights on and off. Dim the lights and let your children have fun pretending to send off flares by making up their own light signals on the walls, floor, and ceiling of your room. Encourage the children to practice flashlight safety by instructing them to hold their flashlights in both hands and to shine their lights away from faces and eyes.

Water Safety

When boating, it is important to make sure there are life jackets available for everyone onboard. One of the responsibilities of the Coast Guard and other rescue boat personnel is to ensure that boaters have the appropriate number of life jackets onboard. Reinforce this safety concept by bringing in one or two child-size life jackets. Show your children how the life jackets are worn, and then help each child take a turn trying one on. Discuss the importance of always wearing a life jacket when around water or in a boat. Consider asking a swimming or boating instructor to talk with your group about water safety. Talk about other boat safety rules, such as keeping your head and limbs inside the boat so you don't fall overboard, wearing shoes or sandals so you don't slip, and staying near a boat that has turned over so that it is easier for a rescuer to see you in the water. Keep the life jackets in your dramatic play area for your children to use in pretend boating play.

Life Preservers

Explain to your children that if you are in a boat or near the water and you see someone in trouble, the best thing to do is to get help. If you can, throw a life preserver or other floating object for the person to hang onto until help arrives.

Talk with the children about things that float. Put items that sink (marbles, metal toy cars, rocks) and items that float (corks, pieces of wood, plastic foam, sponges) in a box. Let your children experiment with the items in your water table to discover which ones sink and which ones float. If you wish, encourage your children to predict if the items will sink or float before putting them into the water.

Extension: Bring in a life preserver and other floats such as kickboards and water wings for your children to explore.

Fire Pump

Explain to your children that most harbors have fireboats that help to put out fires in places fire trucks can't reach. Fireboats are equipped with pumpers and hoses that pump water out of the ocean or sea to put out fires on ships, bridges, and docks. Make the following fireboat for your children to use in your water table. First, thoroughly clean the spray pump from a squirt bottle or household cleaner bottle. Poke the strawlike attachment through the middle of a sponge or rectangular piece of plasticfoam. Place the fireboat in a tub full of water. Show the children how to squeeze the nozzle to pump out the water.

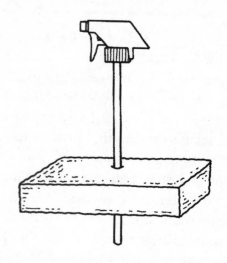

Color Squirt

Collect toy boats of different colors and put them in your water table. Provide your children with squirt bottles. Invite the children to pretend that there are fires on boats of different colors. Call out the color of a boat, such as a blue boat. Have the children use their squirt bottles to squirt water on only the blue boats. Call out the names of other colors of boats and let the children squirt them. Continue while interest lasts.

Fireboat Spray Art

Fill squirt bottles or toys with diluted tempera paint, or water that has been colored with food coloring. Let the children use their squirt toys to squirt water on white paper or cloth. Let the paper or cloth dry overnight. Display the Fireboat Spray Art on a wall or bulletin board.

Rescue Raisins

Large ships carry small boats called lifeboats. There should be enough lifeboats onboard a ship to rescue all of the passengers and crew members during an emergency. Set out small bowls and boxes of raisins. Have your children pretend that the bowls are lifeboats and the raisins are ship passengers. Make up simple math problems for your children to answer using these materials. For example, you might give each child two bowls and tell the children that the lifeboats hold just three passengers apiece. How many people can be rescued? Encourage the children to use their problem-solving skills to find the answer. Guide them toward putting three raisins in each bowl and then counting the total amount of raisins.

Sailboats

Catch the Wind

Explain to your children that sailboats move through the water with the force of the wind. Pieces of fabric called *sails* are attached to *masts* (upright poles) on the boat to catch the wind and make the boat move. On a windy day, bring in an old bed sheet and set it on the ground. Have your children hold onto the edges of the sheet. Tell them that they are going to use the sheet like a sail to "catch" some wind. Then have them lift up the sheet. Encourage the children to move in different directions to see how much wind they can catch. Point out how the middle of the sheet moves in different ways depending on where the wind hits it. For example, sometimes the wind may make the sheet arch in the middle. Other times the sheet may ripple or flatten.

Which Way Is It Blowing?

To steer a sailboat, you need to know the direction of the wind. Invite your children to come up with ideas for finding out in what direction the wind is blowing. Help the children carry out their wind experiments by providing materials and books about the wind. You might introduce directional words such as *north*, *south*, *east*, and *west*.

Extension: Hang a windsock outdoors. Let your children observe the windsock in different types of weather.

Sail Craft

Give each of your children a plastic lid, a construction paper sail shape, a straw, and a small ball of modeling dough. Let the children decorate their sail shapes with crayons and attach them to their straws with masking tape. Then have them put their modeling dough balls in the middle of their lids and stick their straws in their modeling dough. Let the children sail their sailboats in a sink, a wading pool, or a dishpan.

Lung Powered

Provide your children with toy sailboats to sail in your water table. (If you wish, have the children use their Sail Crafts, or invite them to bring sailboats from home.) Encourage the children to use their own wind power to move the boats from one end of the water table to the other by blowing on the boats or generating wind with paper fans. Have them experiment with blowing or fanning at different angles and directions, such as on top of the boat, behind the boat, level with the boat, and from side to side. Which direction makes the boat move faster?

Sailboat Fingerplay

Recite the following poem out loud and have your children act out the motions.

Here's my little sailboat,
> *(Place elbow in palm of hand.)*

Blowing in the wind.
> *(Move arm back and forth.)*

First it's tipping this way,
> *(Bend arm to the right.)*

Then it's tipping that way.
> *(Bend arm tot he left.)*

Now it's going forward.
> *(Bend arm forward.)*

Now it's going back.
> *(Bend arm backward.)*

Polly R. Reedy

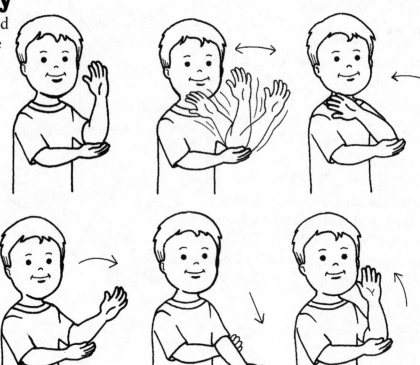

Sailing Away

Play some airy classical music such as Telemann's *Air Suite in D* or soft pop music such as Christopher Cross's *Sailing.* Have your children pretend they are sailboats sailing in the wind. Invite them to sail across the room. Is the wind blowing strongly or softly? Are they moving fast or slow? Where are they sailing?

When the music is over, have the children talk about their sailing journeys.

Sail Match

Cut several rectangular boat shapes out of different colors of felt. Cut several triangular sail shapes out of matching colors of felt. Place the boat shapes on a flannelboard and the sail shapes in a pile next to it. Let your children take turns selecting a sail shape and placing it above the matching boat shape.

Variation: To turn this matching game into a math game, number the boat shapes with numerals and the sail shapes with corresponding amounts of dots.

Extension: Invite your children to look for rectangular and triangular objects around your room.

Celery Boats

Cut celery stalks into 4-inch sections. Fill each section with a spreadable food, such as peanut butter, cream cheese, almond butter, or humus. Add a pretzel mast. Cut small sail shapes out of typing paper. Carefully poke two holes in each sail, and put them on the masts. Have the children remove the paper sails before eating their boats.

Did You Ever See a Sailboat?

Sung to: "Did You Ever See a Lassie?"

Did you ever see a sailboat,

A sailboat, a sailboat?

Did you ever see a sailboat

Set sail in the wind?

When the wind blows, the boat goes

Forward and backward.

Did you ever see a sailboat

Set sail in the wind?

Diane Thom

Submarines

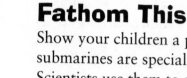

Fathom This

Show your children a picture of a submarine. Explain that submarines are special boats that can travel underwater. Scientists use them to study the ocean floor and to find out how deep it is. They measure the ocean depth in *fathoms*. Ask your children how big they think a fathom might be. Then approximate the length of a fathom by extending your arms out from your sides. Explain that the distance between your hands is approximately one fathom. (A fathom is 6 feet.) Submarines can travel hundreds of fathoms under the sea.

Mark off fathoms on a long rope by tying a series of knots 6 feet apart. String the rope between two chairs or pieces of equipment in the play yard. Pretend one chair is the ocean's surface and the other is the ocean floor. Recite the rhyme "Dive, Dive" while children take turns walking along the rope, grasping each knot to mark off the fathoms.

Dive, Dive

One fathom, two fathoms, three fathoms, four,

My sub dives to the ocean floor.

Way down there my sub will be

Many fathoms under the sea.

Four fathoms, three fathoms, two fathoms, one,

My sub floats back up toward the sun.

Way up there my sub will be

Floating high on the big blue sea.

Durby Peterson

Heavy-Duty Hull

Demonstrate that a submarine needs a strong outer shell, called a *hull*, to keep the water out. The hull is made of strong, thick steel. Set out a gallon of bottled water and let your children attempt to pick it up. Then set out a thin cardboard tube and a metal flashlight (with batteries removed) to represent two different hulls. First set the bottled water on top of the cardboard tube. Then set it on the metal flashlight. Let your children observe that the weak "submarine" gets crushed, but not the strong one. Explain that when a real submarine is deep under the ocean, many gallons of water press down on it, so it needs a very strong hull.

Diving Fun

Explain that people who live and work in submarines are called submariners. When submariners want their submarine to dive, they let in ocean water to make the submarine heavy enough to drift downward. When the submariners want to rise to the surface, they empty the water and float upward.

Let your children investigate this concept. Set several empty margarine containers (with lids on) by your water table. Ask your children to try to make them sink. Then have your children open the lids and fill the tubs up with water. Do they sink more easily when full? Let your children continue experimenting with their submarine tubs.

Periscope Song
Sung to: "The Paw-Paw Patch"

Put the periscope down.

We are going under.

Put the periscope down.

We are going under.

Put the periscope down.

We are going under,

Under water in the deep blue sea.

Put the periscope up.

What's on the surface?

Put the periscope up.

What's on the surface?

Put the periscope up.

What's on the surface?

What's on the surface of the deep blue sea?

Durby Peterson

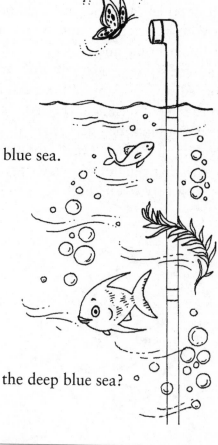

Playful Periscopes

If possible, show your children a picture of a periscope. Explain that submariners look through a periscope to see ships on the surface of the water. Let them know that a submarine can remain under water while the periscope is up above the water, giving the submariners a view of what is going on up there. As you sing "Periscope Song," have your children squat down low for the first verse, then stand up tall and look around for the second verse. Have them name some things they see.

Underwater Art

Add several drops of blue food coloring to the water in your water table. Have the children crumple large coffee filters into balls and hold them under the water for about a minute. Remove the crumpled filters, flatten them, and spread them out on a toweled surface. Let the children decorate their dry blue filters with pictures or stickers of undersea creatures.

Variation: Submerge the filters in a second color, such as deep green or purple, if desired.

I See You!

Collect a round oatmeal container for each of your children. Remove the lids and set aside. Poke one small hole halfway up the side of each container. Have each child tip his or her container on its side and insert a flexible drinking straw into the hole. Show them how to bend the straw at a 45-degree angle so it resembles a periscope. Invite your children to put one hand inside their submarine to turn the periscope first one direction and then another. Set some toy boats on a table. Your children will enjoy making their submarines dive below the surface (under the table) and peek at the ships above.

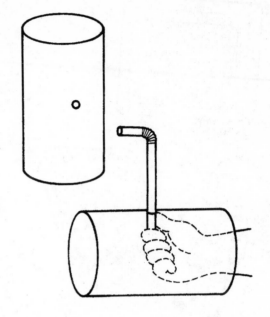

Sending Sonar

Explain that when a submarine is deep underwater, the people inside cannot see where they are going. They use waves of sound, called *sonar*, to tell what is in their path. Sonar equipment sends out a high-pitched sound. The sound bounces off other ships or even fish and comes back to the submarine, letting the submariners know that something is there.

To demonstrate, ask one child to stand with his back to the others while they quietly tiptoe to one corner of the room. Then ask the single child to clap his or her hands once. Have the others clap once in response. Without looking, let the single child try pointing to the corner where he or she thinks the other children are. Continue play until each child has sent out "sonar."

Long Time at Sea

Your children may be surprised to learn that modern submarines can stay underwater for months at a time. For this reason, it is important for the crew to have some things to do just for fun. Subs are often equipped with such things as a game room, a television, and a small library. Ask your children what they might bring if they were going on a long submarine voyage.

What to Bring?

Sung to: "Oh, Susanna"

If I lived on board a submarine
Without much room to run,
I would bring with me a couple things
And people just for fun.

Chorus:
On a sub,
I'd bring the things I like—
Some games and toys, some picture books,
My blanket, and my trike.

I would bring my mom and bring my dad,
And little brother, too.
I would bring my favorite teddy bear
And a real small car or two.

Durby Peterson

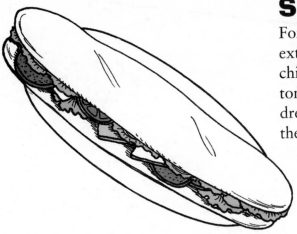

Sub Sandwich

For snacktime, prepare a submarine sandwich on an extra-long sandwich bun. Fill it with ingredients your children will enjoy, such as cheese, cold cuts, lettuce, and tomatoes. Before slicing a serving for each of your children, ask the group to look at the whole sandwich. Can they guess why it is called a submarine sandwich?

My Submarine

Sung to: "For He's a Jolly Good Fellow"

My submarine is a sandwich.

My submarine is a sandwich.

My submarine is a sandwich.

Now watch how my submarine dives!

It dives down to my tum.

It dives and I say, "Yum!"

My submarine is a sandwich.

Now watch how my submarine dives!

Durby Peterson

Submerged in Books

Check your local library for these and other books about submarines:

Sally's Submarine, by Joan Anderson, Illustrated by George Ancona, Morrow, 1995.

Submarines, by Michael Green, Capstone Press, 1998.

Submarines and Other Underwater Craft, by Harvey Weiss, Crowell, 1990. (Though this book is designed for older readers, preschoolers will enjoy the many illustrations of underwater vessels.)

On the Tracks

City Trains

City Train Transition

City trains, including subways, elevated trains, and monorails, make big cities livable. Whether they run above the ground or below the ground, these trains make it easy for many people to travel from place to place inside the city very quickly.

At movement time, have your children practice moving like city trains. To move like a subway, have the children crouch down low to the ground as they walk. To move like an elevated train, have the children walk on tiptoes. For a monorail, encourage the children to try hopping on one foot.

Subway Snake

Sung to: "Sing a Song of Sixpence"

Riding in a big snake.

That makes a rattle sound,

Slither through the city,

Then plunge beneath the ground.

Faster, through the darkness,

But I'm not scared because

My snake is a subway train—

That's all it ever was.

Heather Tekavec

Subway Ride

Make signs that say Subway Station, and set them up around the room. Then line up a small group of children to form a subway train. Position the rest of the children at different subway stations. Start the subway train traveling around the room. Call out "Subway Station" when you want the train to stop at one of the stations. Each time it stops, select one or more children to enter or exit the train, varying the number of passengers each time. Encourage all of the children to help you count how many passengers are now on the train.

El Tracks

Elevated trains are trains that run above the city on raised or elevated tracks. Elevated trains are often called *els*. The advantage of being above the ground is that they aren't stopped by, and they don't stop, pedestrian and street traffic.

Provide your children with wooden or plastic train track, toy trains, and various building materials, such as blocks, modeling clay, craft sticks, and small boxes. Invite them to work together to figure out how to use these materials to make an elevated train. Have them develop a firm plan of action before they build. Encourage them to find their own solutions to the problems they may experience as they carry out their building plan.

Variation: Have your children build an elevated train in the sandbox using damp sand.

Above and Below

Make stamp pads by placing folded paper towels inside small trays. Pour tempera paint on top of the towels. Then set out pieces of light-colored construction paper and wooden or plastic train track. Let each child dip a piece of train track into tempera paint. Have the children use the train track as a stamp to print a line of track onto the paper. Invite the children to make a subway train track or an elevated train track by orienting the track near the top or the bottom of the paper. If you wish, provide your children with train stickers and collage materials. Encourage them to complete their subway or elevated train scene using the stickers and other materials to make a cityscape. Or let them draw a subway or elevated train scene using markers and crayons.

Monorail Fun

Monorails are trains that use just one rail rather than two. Trains on monorails either hang down from their single rail or straddle it like a person riding a horse.

Bring in pictures of monorails for your children to look at. Then let them build their own simple monorail. Set out a length of two by four and several small shoeboxes. Let the children put their toy figures in the boxes and give them a ride on their monorail.

Just One

Celebrate the number 1 today. Look around your room to locate items you may have one of, such as one trash can, one clock, and one window. Find out how many only children you have in your group. Have the children point to parts of their body that come in 1s, such as one head, one nose, one mouth, one chin, one tongue, and one heart. Talk about other words that mean or imply one, such as *single, unique, only, mono, alone,* and *solo.*

Magnetic Trains

Some trains don't ride on a track, but are pushed or pulled forward using high-strength magnetic motors. Because there is no friction from wheels or rails, these trains can travel nearly 300 miles per hour. They stop and change speed by varying the magnetic current supplied to the motors.

Make a mini-magnetic train for your children to explore. First, find a sturdy box lid. Use a felt tip marker to draw a track or guideway on the top of the lid. Have your children pretend that a metal washer is a magnetic train. Then place the washer at the start of the track. Show the children how to hold a strong magnet under the box lid to make the washer move. Encourage the children to stay on the track as they move the washer from one end of the track to the other.

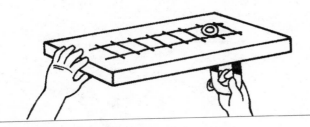

Magnetic Magic

Bring in two strong magnets. Explain to your children that magnets have two sides, or poles. Show your children how the magnets stick together (attract) when their opposite sides (poles) face together. Demonstrate how they move away from each other (repel) when the same sides face together. The same magical magnetic force that repels the two magnets can move a train down a track.

Pair off your children and have them pretend that they are magnets with opposite poles that are attracted to one another. Call out the names of body parts, and have the pairs stick these parts together, such as elbow to elbow, leg to leg, or hand to belly. When you call out "Magnets repel!" encourage the children to unstick themselves and find a new partner.

More Magnetic Fun

Bring a variety of magnets into your classroom, including refrigerator magnets, handheld magnet wands, adhesive magnetic strips, and extra-strong magnets found in hardware stores. The following are suggestions for further magnet exploration.

- Fill a box with a variety of small toys and household items. Have the children use a strong magnet to sort the contents of the box into piles of magnetic and nonmagnetic items.

- Give each of your children a magnet and have them hunt for magnetic surfaces around your room. (Make sure computers are off-limits around strong magnets.)

- Test the strength of several different magnets by charting the amount of small metal items, such as paper clips, each can pick up.

- Let your children make magnetic collages by decorating non-aluminum baking sheets with small magnets, including colored magnets, magnetic letters and numbers, and refrigerator magnets.

- Use magnetic letters to teach your children how to spell their names.

Elevators & Escalators

Elevator Answers

Invite your children to share with you what they know about elevators. Where have they seen them (hotels, shopping centers, apartments, office buildings)? What are they used for (to carry things up and down, to move heavy loads)? How many children have been in an elevator? What did they do to make it go up or down (pressed buttons or arrows, talked into a microphone, gave a floor number to an elevator operator)? What types of things have they seen being moved by elevators (people, luggage, wheelchairs, boxes)? Do your children have questions about what an elevator is and how it works? What can your group do to find the answers?

How Elevators Work

Elevators go up and down with the help of a balance system called a *counterweight*. Help your children understand how a counterweight works with this balance activity.

Make a two-pan balance scale for your children by cutting the middle section out of the bottom part of a wire coat hanger, using wire cutters. Cover the sharp ends of the cuts with masking tape, and bend them up slightly. Punch two holes across from each other in the rims of two paper cups, and make a hanger for each cup by tying on a 6-inch piece of string. Hang the cups from the cut-off ends. Balance the top of the coat hanger on your finger, a hook, or a doorknob.

Designate one cup as the elevator and one as the counterweight. Give your children same-size coins or metal washers. Have them place the same amount of coins or washers into each cup. What happens? Then have them add washers to the elevator cup. Now what happens? How would things change if they took washers away?

Skyscraper Art

Explain to your children that elevators are found in buildings that have more than one floor. The invention of the elevator made it possible to build tall buildings with many levels. These tall buildings are called skyscrapers. Show your children pictures of skyscrapers and other large city buildings such as apartment buildings, hospitals, and hotels. Talk about what skyscrapers look like.

Prepare small boxes, such as gelatin boxes or small milk cartons, by covering them with dark-colored construction paper. Then have the children snip or tear strips of light-colored construction paper into rectangles of different sizes. Let them glue the paper rectangles all over the boxes for skyscraper window and doors.

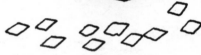

Elevator Movement

Talk with your group about elevators and how they carry people to different floors or levels of a building. Then show your children how to move their bodies at different levels. For example, a first level might be crouching or lying down on the floor. A second level might be bending over at the waist or standing on knees. A third level might be standing on tiptoe or raising arms to the sky. Once your children are comfortable with these levels, have them pretend they are on an elevator. Call out different levels or floors for them to move to.

Elevator Number Board

Collect ten caps from gallon orange juice or milk containers. Number the caps from 1 to 10 using a permanent marker. Then glue them onto a wooden board or piece of heavy cardboard. Invite your children to pretend that the board controls an elevator. Have the children take turns being elevator operators. Call out a number (for the floor you would like to go to) and let the elevator operator search for the correct button.

Variation: Use the elevator board to play a fun number game. Have the children line up all facing you while you hold the elevator board. Point to a number. Have them take that many steps.

Up or Down

Explain to your children that elevators can move only two ways: up or down. Often when you wait outside of an elevator door, lighted arrows show you which way the elevator is moving.

Cut several small arrows out of felt. Position the arrows on your flannelboard to make an up-and-down arrow pattern. Walk your children through the pattern, stopping at each arrow to ask if the elevator would go up or down. Challenge older children to continue the pattern using additional arrows. Invite them to create their own up-and-down elevator patterns.

Variation: If you wish, use arrows of different colors for color patterning activities.

escalator   elevator   stairs

Alike and Different

Show your children pictures of escalators, elevators, and stairways. As a group, compare these three different ways to get from one floor to the other in a building. In what ways do they look and work alike? In what ways do they look and work differently? If you wish, divide a long piece of butcher paper into three sections to make a comparison chart. At the top of one section write the word "escalator" and draw a picture of an escalator underneath. Do the same in the other sections for the words "elevator" and "stairs." Then ask your children questions such as, Which would you use if you were in a running mood? Which would you use if you wanted to go to the top of the building very quickly? Which would you use if you were carrying something heavy? Which would you use if your legs were tired? If your leg was hurt or broken, which one would you use? Have the children answer by placing a mark or a sticker under the section of their choice.

Extension: Take a field trip to a building or shopping center and show your children escalators, elevators, and stairs. Then do this activity again. Did the answers change?

My Escalator

Sung to: "Kookaburra"

The stairs are moving under my feet.
  (Tilt body back and bounce knees up and down, putting one hand on an imaginary railing.)

I'm climbing without walking, isn't that neat?

My escalator, my escalator takes me to the top of the store.
  (Reach hands up to the sky.)

The steps can carry me down again.
  (Tilt body forward and bounce up and down, with hand on railing.)

They fold down flat when they reach the end.
  (Clap hands at the word "flat.")

My escalator, my escalator takes me down once more.
  (Reach hands down to ground.)

Replace *store* with another type of building that might have an escalator, such as an *airport* or a *hotel*.

Author Unknown

Train Station

Happy Tracks Train Station

Loading Platform

Magazines

Tickets

Train Schedules

Arrivals

Departures

Our Train Station

Invite your children to help you set up a train station in the home-life area. Help them think about what a train station is like by reading them related books or providing them with pictures. Talk about some of your own experiences in train stations, and encourage the children to relate any experiences they may have had. Then help the children make a list of the equipment they want their train station to have. Guide their thinking by asking them questions. Does it have a ticket booth or a loading platform? Will it include a store for buying small items to read or eat on the train? Will there be a place for luggage? Encourage them to come up with questions of their own. Together, think of ways to find out the answers. Help the children come up with ideas for making or collecting the items that they will need to complete their train station.

Variation: Instead of a passenger train station, invite your children to set up a freight yard or a city subway station.

Train Names

Some vehicles, such as boats and trains, have names. Train names usually tell something about their destination or route. For example, a train that travels next to the ocean might be named Coast Starlight. Let your children make up names for the trains that arrive and depart from their station. Write the names on a large poster to put up in their station.

Variation: Invite your children to make up a name for their train station. Write the name on a piece of posterboard and hang it above their play area.

Rockin'
Roller

Travel Time

Train stations publish lists of arrival and departure times for all of the trains. Try to gather a few of these listings from your local train station. Help your children use the timetables to figure out how many days or hours it would take to travel from your city to a city far away.

Down to the Station

Take your group to your local train station. Discuss what goes on at the station. What kinds of services are provided? Have the children help you make a list. Use your list to help your children in planning a train station they can set up in your room. If possible, make arrangements for the children to take a short ride on one of the trains during your train station field trip.

Ticket Booth

Help your children set up a ticket booth for their station. Cut various-colored pieces of construction paper into strips for your children to use as tickets. They may want to gather some play money and a cash box or shoebox to use at their ticket booth.

Magazine Stand

Bring in a selection of books and magazines. Let your children set them out on a table to make their Magazine Stand. Supply play money and a cash box or small shoebox. Don't forget to include travel magazines and a couple of books about trains.

Snack Bar

Help your children set up a small snack bar in their train station. They could sell juice boxes, crackers, and carrot or celery sticks. Let them set up their Snack Bar on a table. Include play money and a cash box or shoebox.

Train Platform

The platform is the area outside the station where the trains stop and let people on and off. Porters work on the platform, helping people put their luggage on and off of the train. They often have wheeled carts to help them transport the suitcases and other luggage. Have your children decide what they could use outside their station to transport luggage. Provide a few different-sized boxes for the children to use as luggage.

Loading Platform

I've Been Working on the Railroad

I've been working on the railroad,

All the livelong day.

I've been working on the railroad,

Just to pass the time away.

I'm a railroad engineer.

I drive the train up and back.

I sit up front and blow the whistle

And I keep the train on track.

I've been working on the railroad,

All the livelong day.

I've been working on the railroad,

Just to pass the time away.

I'm a railroad conductor.

I'll take your tickets, please.

I will guide you to the platform

So you'll board the train with ease.

I've been working on the railroad,

All the livelong day.

I've been working on the railroad,

Just to pass the time away.

I'm a railroad porter.

I'll take you to your seat.

I'll help carry all your baggage

And make sure your berth is neat.

Adapted Traditional

Down by the Station

Down by the station

Early in the morning,

See the little train cars

All in a row.

See the stationmaster

Turn a little handle.

Chug, chug, chug, chug,

Off they go.

Adapted Traditional

Train Tracks

You might want to discuss train tracks with your children. Provide some reference books about trains, such as those listed below. What are they made of? How are they built? How do people build tracks over mountains?

Set out a model train set and let your children build a railroad track around your room. If a model train set is not available, cut track sections (both straight and curved) out of cardboard or use long, thin wooden blocks.

All Aboard Books

All Aboard Trains, by Mary Harding, Illustrated by Richard Courtney, Price Stern Sloan, 1989.

DK Big Book of Trains, by Christine Heap, DK Publishing, 1998.

Thomas the Tank Engine Series, by W. Awdry, Random House, various years.

Trains

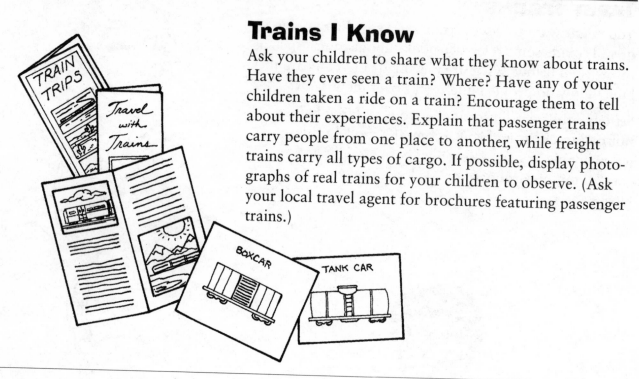

Trains I Know

Ask your children to share what they know about trains. Have they ever seen a train? Where? Have any of your children taken a ride on a train? Encourage them to tell about their experiences. Explain that passenger trains carry people from one place to another, while freight trains carry all types of cargo. If possible, display photographs of real trains for your children to observe. (Ask your local travel agent for brochures featuring passenger trains.)

Choo-Choo Train

Sung to: "Twinkle, Twinkle, Little Star"

As you sing the following song, let your children take turns filling in the blanks.

The train goes chugging up and down,

Carrying _____ from town to town.

It carries _____ and _____ too.

As it goes, it says, "Choo-choo."

The train goes chugging up and down,

Carrying _____ from town to town.

Elizabeth McKinnon

My Favorite Train

Read aloud to your children the favorite childhood classic, *The Little Engine That Could*. Then teach them the following song.

The Wheels on the Train

Sung to: "The Wheels on the Bus"

The wheels on the train go clickety-clack,

Clickety-clack, clickety-clack.

The wheels on the train go clickety-clack,

All along the track.

The engine on the train goes chug, chug, chug;

Chug, chug, chug; chug, chug, chug.

The engine on the train goes chug, chug, chug,

All along the track.

Additional verses: The whistle on the train goes toot, toot, toot; The toys on the train go up and down; The rusty old engine said, "I cannot"; The toys on the train said, "Please, please, please"; The little engine said, "I think I can"; The little engine said, "I thought I could."

Beth Smalley

All Aboard!

Have your children line up at the station (one side of the room). Pretend you are the engineer driving a passenger train. Teach your children to recite the first part of the following rhyme as they wait for the train. Then have one child at a time board the train by holding onto your waist. Together, take a lap around the room or yard as you say the second verse of the rhyme. Then come back around to pick up another passenger. Have each child that boards the train hold onto the shoulders of the child ahead. If you wish, set up an obstacle course with chairs or boxes for the train to weave around.

Chug-A-Chug-Chug

Engineer, engineer,

Stop at the station over here.

Chug-a-chug-chug,

Clackety-clack.

Let's go chugging round the track.

Chug-a-chug-chug,

Clackety-clack.

Let's go chugging all the way back.

Adapted Traditional

Big Moo Choo-Choo

Wash several empty cardboard milk cartons. Turn them into boxcars by pressing down the top flap of each carton. Tape each carton shut so it forms a rectangle. Let your children help wrap each carton in plain brown paper or white butcher paper. (If you wish, wrap one carton in black paper for the engine and another in red for the caboose.) Together, cut out and glue on cardboard wheels. Then connect the boxes with yarn. Let your children take turns driving the train. They will enjoy placing cargo such as small blocks or plastic toys on top of the cars.

Hint: Cut off the top of some boxcars so that cargo can be placed inside.

Boxcar Fun

Set out several cardboard boxes that are big enough for your children to step into. Remove the tops and bottoms. Invite your children to use markers or stickers to decorate each box to look like a train car. Then make a set of suspenders for each carton by attaching two pieces of heavy yarn from front to back. Have your children step inside the boxes and hang the suspenders over their shoulders. Then let them chug around the room in line as a train.

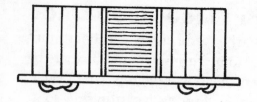

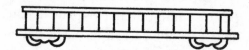

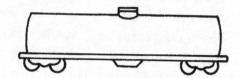

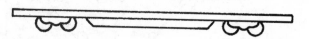

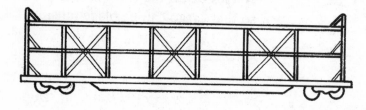

Carrying Cargo

Show your children a picture or detailed drawing of a freight train with different types of cars. (See illustration.) Point out the boxcars, gondola cars, tanker cars, flatcars, rack cars, and livestock cars. Talk with your children about the type of freight each car might carry, such as appliances, furniture, stone, gravel, coal, milk, fruit, lumber, automobiles, and cattle. Encourage your children to pretend they are stopped at a railroad crossing, watching the train pass. Together, sing the following song and then count all the cars in the picture.

Count the Cars

Sung to: "The Farmer in the Dell"

Let's count the railroad cars.

Let's count the railroad cars
Rolling along the track.

Let's count the railroad cars.

Count boxcars that you see

And flatcars, one, two, three,

The engine and the red caboose.

Come count the cars with me!

Durby Peterson

Then and Now

Show a picture of an old-fashioned steam engine and a modern diesel or electric locomotive for your children to compare. How are the engines alike? How are they different? Explain that the first train engines were powered by steam. To make steam, the engineer heated water by burning wood or coal. Most modern trains have diesel or electric engines. Explain that modern train engines can travel much faster than the old steam engines. Many can even travel faster than a small airplane.

Take the Train

For a fun way to move your children from one area to another, ask them to line up as train cars and "hook" onto the child in front of them. Have them chug along from place to place. You might lay two parallel lines of masking tape on the floor for train tracks. Can your children stay on the tracks as they go?

Speedy Snack Express

For snacktime, line up a row of crackers on each child's plate. Top each cracker (or car of the train) with a small slice of cheese or lunchmeat. Add sliced black olives for wheels. Tell your children that they are passengers on a train and it's time to go into the "dining car" to eat. After their snack, have your children pretend to go to the "sleeper car" for rest time.

This Little Train

Sung to: "This Old Man"

This little engine,

It is black.

It goes chugging down the track.

With a chug-chug, toot-toot,

Hear the whistle blow.

This little train goes chugging home.

This little car,

It is blue.

It goes chugging right by you.

With a chug-chug, toot-toot,

Hear the whistle blow.

This little train goes chugging home.

Additional verses: It is pink, it goes chugging quick as a wink; It is yellow, it goes chugging, whistling hello; It is green, it goes chugging full of steam; It is purple, it goes chugging, carrying people; It is white, it goes chugging out of sight; This caboose, it is red, it goes chugging off to bed.

Joan Giesbrecht

Flannelboard Fun

Use the patterns on page 245 as a guide for cutting out of felt a black engine shape, a red caboose shape, and six boxcar shapes as described in the song below. Then let your children take turns putting the shapes on a flannelboard as you sing "This Little Train." When all the shapes are in place, count them together.

Train Pattern

Use with the activity on page 244.

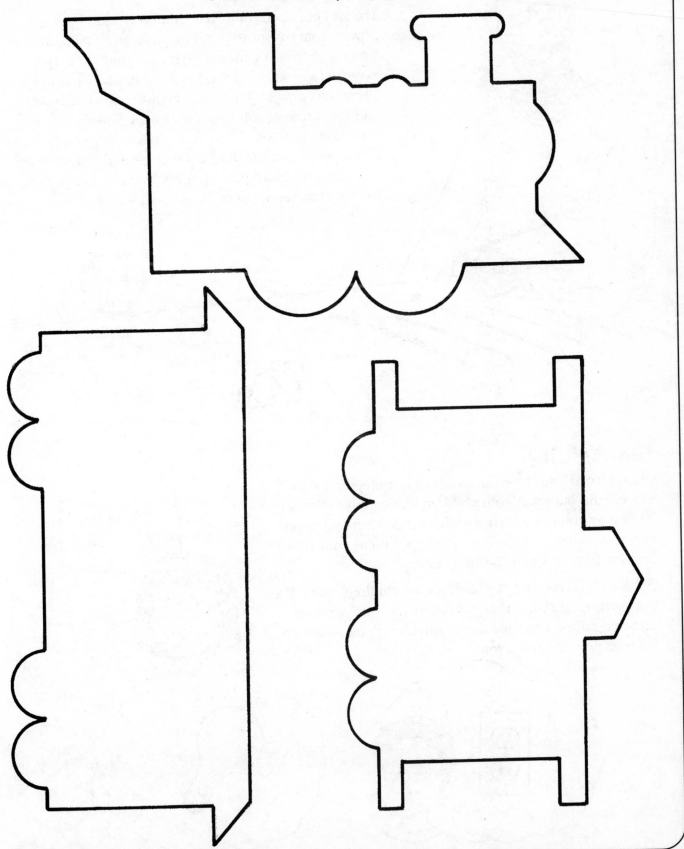

Trolleys

All Wired Up

Trolleys are open trains that run on tracks. They get power from overhead wires or underground conductors. Bring in different gauges of wire for your children to explore (wire can be found at most hardware stores and electronics shops). Point out the different sizes of wire, and the different colors of covering, or insulation, that surround the wire. Where have your children seen wires? If you wish, provide your children with different lengths of fishing wire and pipe cleaners, and encourage them to use these materials to make wire sculptures.

Electricity

Electricity helps power the motor of a trolley so it will move. Find out what your children know about electricity. They may connect electricity with lights, electrical appliances, switches, and sockets. Then go around your room looking for items that use electricity.

Follow up this activity by having your children cut or tear out pictures of things that use electricity from catalogs and magazines. Examine the pictures, and talk about what each item is used for.

Stop and Go Game

Explain to your children that trolleys have overhead cords that you must pull down when you want to get off. The cord is attached to a bell that will ring to let the driver know to stop. Talk with your children about things that signal people to stop, such as red lights and stop signs on roads and whistles from referees at sports events. What words or actions do the children use when they want to stop?

Make up a group stopping signal, such as holding out your arm, yelling "Cut!" into a megaphone, or turning the lights on and off. Then have everyone move around the room. If you wish, play music to keep everyone going. Anytime someone wants to stop, encourage them to use the group stop signal.

Trolley Bells Ring

Sung to: "Rock-a-bye Baby"

Cling, clang, cling, clang, the trolley bells ring,
  (*Pretend to ring bells.*)

While overhead the sparks zip, zip, zing!
  (*Point overhead.*)

Ride on the trolley, up the hilltop,
  (*Walk hands up, like climbing a hill.*)

Then pull on the cord, the trolley will stop.
  (*Pull hand down, then thrust hand out to stop.*)

If you wish, let one or more children ring bells throughout the song. You might also want to place a bell in your block area to encourage trolley play.

Carol Gnojewski

Group Trolley Line

To keep people interested in riding trolleys, some trolley companies built their lines around natural wonders such as lakes and rock formations. Some even constructed amusement parks that could be reached only by trolley.

Spread butcher paper on the floor, and secure the edges with tape. Then provide your children with paint and wooden or plastic train track, and have them use the track to stamp out a trolley line in the middle of the paper. While the trolley line dries, discuss as a group what you might see as you travel along the line on your class trolley. Set out art materials such as crayons and markers, and help the children draw scenery on both sides of the track. Display your Trolley Line mural for parents and other visitors, or let the children use it for play with toy trains and action figures.

Extension: Discuss the difference between something that is natural, and something that is man-made.

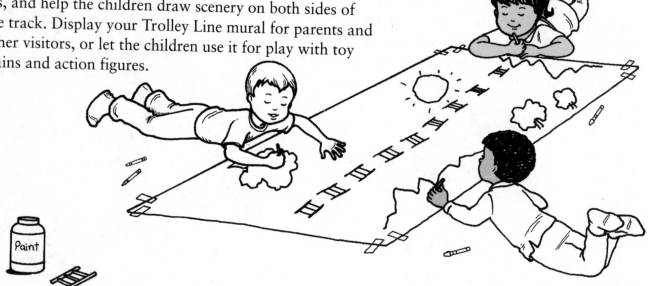

Trolley Color Match

Explain to your children that trolley cars have small colored-glass windows that hang just below the roof. Years ago when trolleys were popular, people who couldn't read used the color of the glass to help them find the car that would take them where they wanted to go.

Using the trolley pattern on page 249, cut five trolley cars from different colors of felt or construction paper. Then use the trolley riders pattern on the same page to cut 15 people from felt or construction paper of corresponding colors. Have the children match the people to the correct cars.

Extension: Use the trolley and trolley riders patterns for math and counting activities.

Trolley Color-Matching Patterns

Use with the activity on page 248.

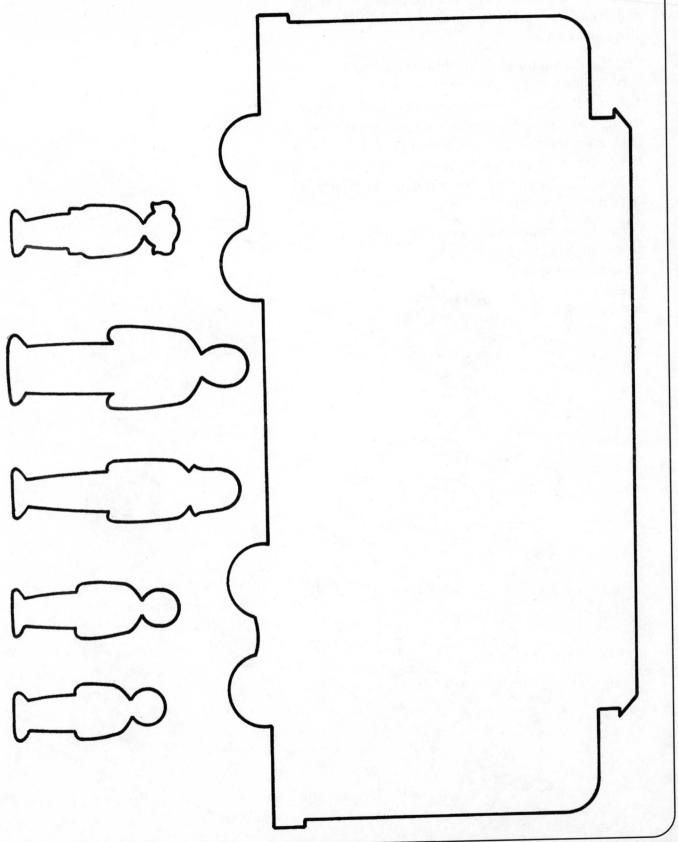

Tunnels

Tunnel Discovery

A tunnel is a passageway that cars, trains, and other vehicles use to travel underground, underwater, and through mountains.

Create a mountain tunnel in your sandbox. Tie string or heavy twine around a toy car (or pass the string through the car if its doors or windows open). Thread the car through a cardboard paper towel tube and lay it on the sand. Position the car at one end of the tube while the end of the string hangs out the other. Then help your children build a mountain over the tunnel. Make sure to leave the ends uncovered.

When the mountain is complete, carefully pull the car through the tunnel. Ask your children to predict whether it will come out the other end clean or dirty.

Passing Through

Cut a tunnel shape out of black construction paper for each of your children. Collect real pebbles, or give the children pieces of gray construction paper and have them cut or tear them into rocklike shapes. Help the children glue the pebbles or paper shapes around the outside edge of their paper tunnel. Then provide the children with white or yellow crayons. Encourage them to use the crayons to draw a bright circle of light shining out of the tunnel.

Let the children decide what type of vehicle is traveling through their paper tunnel. Why is it important for the drivers of these vehicles to turn on lights as they pass through them? (Because tunnels are dark, lights let others know they are there.) Invite your children to recount any experiences they have had riding through tunnels.

Tunnel Sounds

Provide your children with a variety of tubes. Try to find tubes of sizes, made from diverse materials such as plastic, cardboard, and metal. (Visit your local hardware store for a wide selection of tubes.) Let the children take turns making train sounds through the tubes. Then have them make train sounds without the tubes. Were the sounds louder or softer through a tube? Which tube makes the best noise?

Different Tunnels

Use chairs, tables, appliance boxes, and blocks to make four or five tunnels around your room. Vary the length, width, and degree of darkness inside of each tunnel. Let your children pretend to be trains and cars exploring the tunnels for a while. Then gather together to discuss which tunnels are the longest, the shortest, the darkest, the widest, and the easiest to crawl through.

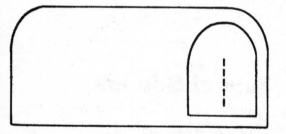

Tunnel Fun

Using the illustrations at left as your guides, cut a tunnel out of stiff gray or black paper. Create a slit where indicated for the tunnel opening. Then use the boxcar pattern to make five boxcars out of different colors of paper. Glue the boxcars in a row onto a thin strip of cardboard. As you recite "Five Little Boxcars" (page 253) to your children, send the boxcars, one at a time, into the back of the tunnel. On the last line, pull the train out the other end. Encourage your children to make tooting or chugging noises as the boxcars reappear.

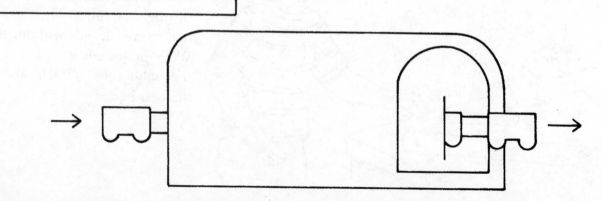

Five Little Boxcars

Five little boxcars going on a trip.

The first one says, "There's a tunnel ahead."

The second one says, "It's awfully black."

The third one says, "Stay on the track."

The fourth one says, "Go very slow."

The fifth one says, "Not far to go."

Then it's quiet in the tunnel till the boxcars shout,

"Blow the whistle, we're coming out!"

Heather Tekavec

Tunnels Everywhere

Sung to: "Hush, Little Baby"

Ants build tunnels in little dirt mounds,
   (Wiggle your fingers to represent crawling ants.)

Moles dig tunnels underground.
   (Pretend to dig in the ground with a shovel.)

But the biggest tunnel I've ever spied
   (Extend your arms out to your sides as far as they'll go.)

Wound through a mountain and out the other side.
   (Weave your arms in and out.)

Heather Tekavec

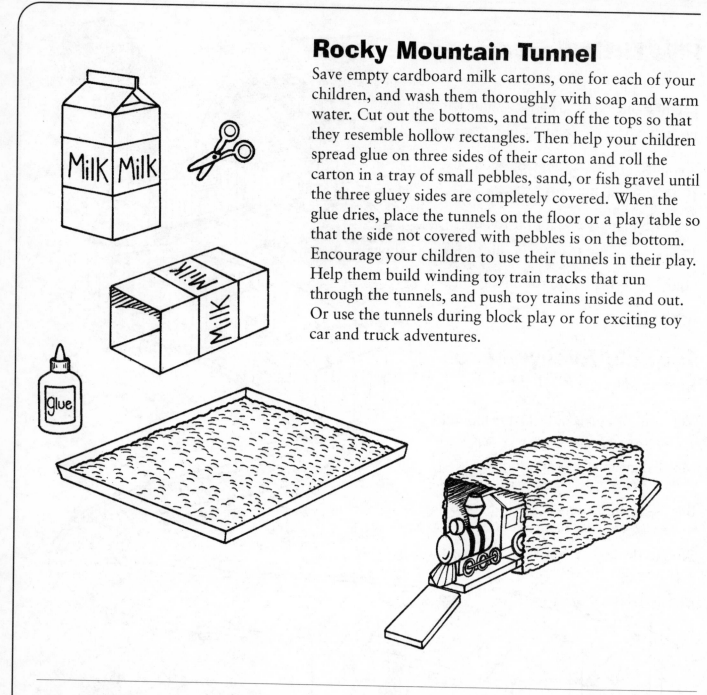

Rocky Mountain Tunnel

Save empty cardboard milk cartons, one for each of your children, and wash them thoroughly with soap and warm water. Cut out the bottoms, and trim off the tops so that they resemble hollow rectangles. Then help your children spread glue on three sides of their carton and roll the carton in a tray of small pebbles, sand, or fish gravel until the three gluey sides are completely covered. When the glue dries, place the tunnels on the floor or a play table so that the side not covered with pebbles is on the bottom. Encourage your children to use their tunnels in their play. Help them build winding toy train tracks that run through the tunnels, and push toy trains inside and out. Or use the tunnels during block play or for exciting toy car and truck adventures.

Apple Tunnel Snack

Halve several apples and generously cut out their cores so that the centers resemble tunnels. Place the apple halves cut-side down on plates or napkins. Give an apple half to each of your children along with a handful of raisins. Show your children how to push raisin "cars" through their apple tunnels.

Tunnel Transition

Divide your children into "boxcars" and "tunnels." Have the tunnels raise their arms to form one long tunnel through which the boxcars can travel. Point the train in the direction of your next activity. During the day, let the children take turns being boxcars and tunnels.

Cardboard Tunnel

Cut off both ends of a large appliance box. Reinforce the box by wrapping tape around its sides. Let your children take turns scooting their riding toys through the Cardboard Tunnel.

On the Snow

Ice Skates

A Smooth Ride

Ice-skating originated in northern countries to help people travel over frozen and ice-covered ground. Skates enable people to move quickly and safely across the ice with little effort. Throughout the day, have your children pretend to wear ice skates. As they move from one activity to another, encourage them to glide across the room in their socks or slippers.

Way Up North

Sung to: "Up on the Housetop"

Way up north where cold winds blow,

Home of frost and wintry snow,

How do the children get around

On the ice and frozen ground?

Glide, glide, glide on their skates,

Over ponds and frozen lakes.

They wear skates to ride, ride, ride

Across the ice to the other side.

Carol Gnojewski

Junior Skaters

Make a mini skating rink by freezing a few inches of water in a plastic tub. Let your children scoot play people along the ice as if they were ice-skating. Play classical music in the background as accompaniment. Encourage the children to wear mittens so their fingers won't get cold as they play with the ice.

Skate Discovery

The first ice skates were made from bones strapped to boots. Today, a steel blade is fitted onto the bottom of each skating boot. Bring in a pair or pairs of figure skates to show your children. When the children handle the skates, make sure that the blades have guards on them to prevent injuries. Point out the sharp metal teeth on the blade near the toe. These are called *toe picks*. They help skaters make spins, jumps, and turns.

Variation: If you can, try to find a pair of hockey skates, speed skates, and figure skates. Help the children compare the different blades (speed skates have long flat blades, hockey skates have shorter blades with curves, figure skates have very curved blades with toe picks). Explain that the different lengths and curves help people who skate with them do different things. (The speed skate is designed to move very fast in one direction, the hockey skate is designed for speed in all directions, and the figure skate is curved so that jumps and spins can be performed.)

Skater's Marks

Many people associate skating with ice dancing or figure skating routines set to music. Give each of your children some paper and two crayons. Have the children pretend that the paper is the ice, and the crayons are the skate blades. Let them "dance" their crayons on the paper to make marks. Have them hold both crayons in one hand as if they were ice-skating. (Or use masking tape to secure the two crayons together.) Play classical music and encourage the children to make long, swirling marks. Play up-tempo jazzy music for shorter, faster marks.

Variation: To provide a larger work area, tape butcher paper to the floor.

For More Fun: Consult your local librarian for books and videos about figure skating.

Figure Eight

Skaters often practice skating in large loops that resemble the number eight. Use tape to make a large figure 8 on the floor of your room. Have the children walk along it one at a time. If you wish, let them pretend to move along the figure as if they were wearing skates. Encourage the children who are waiting their turn to count to eight as others walk.

Variation: Take this activity outside with sidewalk chalk.

Winter Ice-skating Scene

Cut two ½-inch strips from a sponge about 2 inches long. Use hot glue to attach them onto the palm side of an old mitten. Make the strips parallel to each other, but slightly staggered so that it looks as if one skate is ahead of the other. Let one of your children at a time put on the mitten and dip it into brightly colored paint to make ice skate blade prints on white paper. If you wish, provide tree stamps or cookie cutters dipped in green paint for the children to add to their scene. Provide glue and coarse salt to sprinkle on as snow.

Learning to Fall

Ice-skating requires good balance to control your movements on the thin blades and slippery surface. One of the first things that beginning skaters are taught is how to fall on the ice without risking an injury. Your children will have fun learning how to fall safely. Spread mats on the floor and show your children how to squat with their arms straight out in front of them. Help them roll backward onto one side of their backside or another. Encourage them not to use their hands and arms as they fall backward.

Hint: Falling backward, instead of leaning forward to catch a fall with your arms, prevents arm and wrist breaks. This is a good way to try to fall whenever you're caught off balance.

Ice Pop Snack

Let your children make and eat ice for a snack! Give each child a small paper cup and a craft stick. Provide a variety of fruit juices, such as apple, orange, grape, pineapple, and lemon. Help the children pour the juice or juices of their choice into their cups. Freeze the juice cups for about one hour, and then have the children stick craft sticks in them. Continue to freeze until each Ice Pop is solid.

Hint: Run a little warm water over the cups to help loosen the pop from the paper.

Sleds

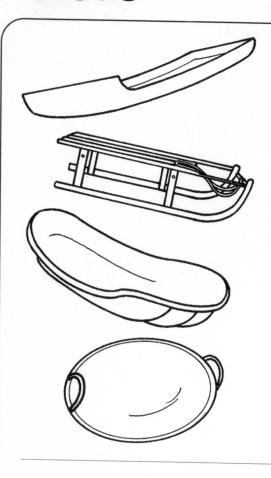

Sled Discovery

For a long, long time, people have been using sleds to move across the ice and snow. The first sleds were probably skins stretched across pieces of wood. Bring in a variety of sturdy sleds for your children to explore, including toboggans, wooden sleds with runners such as Flexible Flyers, and plastic shells or saucers. Talk about the differences and similarities that they see. Some sleds have steel runners that make thin grooved tracks on packed snow. Some have crossbars for steering. Other sleds have flat bottoms with handles on the sides.

Extension: Let your children play with the sleds during free time.

Sled Rides

Attach small pieces of rope to the handles of plastic, flat-bottomed sleds or saucers. Use the ropes to give your children sled rides. Or let the children use the sleds to pull small toys, dolls, and stuffed animals around your room or play yard.

Hint: This activity works best outdoors or on carpeted surfaces. Plastic sleds may scuff vinyl or wood floors.

Sledding Positions

Place cushions under a small slide or ramp. Have your children pretend they are sliding down a hill on a sled. Encourage the children to try different sledding positions, including sliding down while sitting, sliding down on their backs, and sliding down on their stomachs, either face or feet first. Explain that most sleds are steered by shifting your weight (moving side to side) in these positions.

Hint: Be sure to have adult spotters at the bottom of the slide.

Sled Science

Help the children build sledding ramps using blocks and baking sheets. Try to make at least one very low ramp and one very steep ramp. If you wish, dust the ramps with baking soda to make them slippery. Have the children slide their Mini-Sleds down the ramps. Ask them to predict whether their sleds will slide faster on a low ramp or a steep ramp. Try adding small toys to the sleds to see how weight affects sliding speed. Compare the sliding performance of different shapes of sleds, such as round sleds, rectangular sleds, triangular sleds, and square sleds.

Variation: Try this activity with snow or sand at your sensory table. Or, take this activity outside if there is snow on the ground.

Extension: Make a class chart of your scientific sled findings.

Mini-Sleds

Bring in pictures of different types of sleds. Provide your children with paint, glue, craft sticks, wooden blocks, small cardboard boxes (such as pudding boxes) and plastic and metal lids. Have the children use these materials to build their own miniature sleds for sledding play with small action figures.

Tasty Toboggans

A toboggan is a long, narrow, flat-bottomed sled made of thin boards curled upward in front. Its curved front helps the sled glide smoothly over bumps, drifts, and snow mounds. Give each of your children a rectangular strip of commercial or homemade fruit leather (recipe follows). Have the children roll up one side. If you wish, provide O-shaped cereal, granola, or raisins for them to set on their toboggans. Your children will enjoy coasting their toboggans into their mouths.

Fruit Leather

Use a blender to puree 5 cups of peeled and cored fresh fruit. Heat blended fruit in a saucepan until it resembles a thick sauce. Add spices such as cinnamon or nutmeg if desired. Blend heated fruit a second time and pour onto a baking sheet that has been covered with plastic wrap. Spread the pureed fruit evenly over the wrap with a spatula. Bake at 150°F for 8 hours.

Pack It Up

Dogsled races such as the Iditarod in Alaska celebrate travelling at "the speed of dog." The Iditarod is named for the supply route taken by a daring *musher* (dogsled driver) and sled-dog team to deliver medicine to isolated Alaskan communities during an epidemic. A dogsled is packed from back to front, leaving room for the driver in the very front of the sled.

Make a packing list by drawing a rebus of items around your room that you would like to transport from one side of the room to the other. Help your children use the rebus to fill a sled according to the packing list. If you wish, let one child sit in the front of the sled as the musher. Find out how many "sled dogs" it takes to push or pull the packed sled to its destination.

Sled Dogs

Robust, thick-furred dogs, such as Malamutes, Siberian Huskies, and Alaskan Huskies, are working dogs bred to pull sleds laden with supplies and people over wintry, northern terrain. Show your children pictures of sled-dog breeds. Have them compare the sled dogs to other dog breeds. Why might sled dogs have such thick fur?

Sled Dog Song

Sung to: "The Wheels on the Bus"

The driver of the sled cries, "Mush, mush, mush,"

As he steers his team through the ice and slush.

The strong sled dogs will rush, rush, rush,

Racing through the snow.

Behind the driver, in the back,

Food and supplies are tightly packed.

The heavy sled makes long, deep tracks

Sliding through the snow.

Carol Gnojewski

Sleigh Ride Story

Gather your children in a circle and relate the following story. Encourage your children to listen closely and make choices that will aid your telling. Invite them to act out the parts of the story they like best.

It's a cold, wintry night and you are very excited. You are about to go on your first sleigh ride! You will have to dress warmly. You put on your hat and then put on your gloves and wrap a scarf around your neck. As you are buttoning your coat, you hear the ringing of bells—sleigh bells. The sleigh has arrived! You run outside and climb into the sleigh, next to the driver. What kind of sleigh will you ride? Is it a large wooden sleigh or a small metal one? Maybe it's a fanciful sleigh right out of a fairy tale, or is it Santa's sleigh? The driver whistles and the animals begin to move. Are they dogs, horses, or reindeer? How many do you see? You are moving fast, and the wind is nipping at your nose. The snow is drifting higher and higher. You can almost reach out and touch the snow all around you. You start to shiver, so you search the sleigh for a blanket. What other goodies are packed in back? You find your blanket. Under the blanket is a familiar-looking thermos. Who does it belong to? The thermos is very warm. Slowly you unscrew the top. The hot liquid steams and you can smell what's inside. What does your nose think it is? Perhaps it's hot chocolate or spiced apple cider? You pour the drink into the thermos cup. Maybe you should blow on it a bit before you taste it. You take a sip. The warm liquid relaxes you and makes your whole body feel toasty and warm. Happier now, you look around you. Stars are shining brightly in a clear sky. How many stars can you count? You begin to hum a little tune, and the driver hums with you. He lets you take the reins. You are in charge of the sleigh! Do you make the animals go faster, or do you slow down? What do you do to keep the animals going? The driver takes the reins again as you near your home. When the sleigh stops, the driver hands you a bucket of food. The food is not for you. It is a snack for the animals. You reach into your back pocket and pull out a stiff-bristled brush. As the animals eat, you brush them until their coats are soft and glossy. You thank them for your sleigh ride. The animals look sleepy as the driver and sleigh speed away. It is past your bedtime, too. You walk inside your house and stumble to your room and curl up in bed for the night.

Sleigh Sounds

Bells were often added to the harnesses of animals pulling sleighs to add to the charm of riding and to alert passersby. Bring in sleigh bells or jingle bells for your children to experiment with. Let the children tie the bells to their sleds, or use them to accompany Sleighing Songs.

Jingle Bells

Dashing through the snow,

In a one-horse open sleigh.

O'er the fields we go,

Laughing all the way.

Bells on bobtail ring,

Making spirits bright.

What fun it is to ride and sing

A sleighing song tonight.

Jingle bells, jingle bells,

Jingle all the way.

Oh, what fun it is to ride in a one-horse open sleigh.

Jingle bells, jingle bells,

Jingle all the way.

Oh, what fun it is to ride in a one-horse open sleigh.

Traditional

Sleighing Songs

In times gone by, sleigh rides and caroling were winter traditions. Teach your children some wintry carols that involve sleighing, such as "Winter Wonderland," "Sleigh Ride," "Jingle Bells," and "Over the River and Through the Woods."

Over the River and Through the Woods

Over the river and through the woods,

To grandmother's house we go.

The horse knows the way to carry the sleigh

Through the white and drifting snow, oh.

Over the river and through the woods,

Comfy in our sleigh.

We'll sing a song as we glide along,

For this is our sledding day.

Adapted Traditional

Snowmobiles & Snowplows

Vehicle Flip Book

Snowmobiles have an engine for speed and a drive track for traction that enables them to travel over snow and ice-covered areas where other vehicles cannot go. With runners on the bottom and handlebar steering, they look like a combination of a sled and a motorcycle.

Find pictures of different kinds of land, air, water, and snow vehicles from old books, magazines, and catalogs. Mount the pictures on index cards and cover them with clear self-stick paper, if you wish. Then use a hole punch to punch holes in the left-hand side of each picture. Arrange the cards in a ring binder, as shown in the illustration, to make a flipbook with two cards per page. Encourage your children to flip through the book and compare the different vehicles. Where do they travel? How are they steered? What parts do they have in common?

Variation: Cut pictures horizontally in half before mounting them. Arrange them on the ring binder so that each page has a top and bottom half. Your children can then make many different types of vehicles, such as a vehicle with the top half of an airplane, and the bottom half of a snowmobile. What might this vehicle be used for? What would it be called?

Fantasy Snowmobile

Snowmobiles are the limousines or luxury cars of the snow-travel world. Some models have features such as heated handgrips, soft seats, hoods, and tall windshields to block wind and blowing snow.

Have your children design their own fantasy snowmobile. Might it have an ejector button, a robot autopilot, a foot warmer, or an instant hot chocolate maker? Invite the children to let their imagination take over as they think of other special features to add to their design.

Extension: Have older children draw or paint their special snowmobile. Or encourage them to use blocks and other building materials to make a snowmobile model.

On Again–Off Again

Snowmobiles are both on- and off-road vehicles. This means they can travel on both regular roads and highways as well as places where no roads exist. People who own snowmobiles often belong to clubs that sponsor snowmobile trails. Staying on these maintained trails helps prevent accidents and limits environmental disturbances.

Reinforce the opposites *on* and *off* with this pretend play game. Use tape to mark off a trail inside your room. Then have your children pretend they are snowmobiles driving on the snowmobile trail. When you say "On," have the children drive on the taped path. When you say "Off," have them drive about the room, avoiding the taped path.

Variation: Turn music on and off instead of calling to your children.

Noisy or Nice

Snowmobiles can be very loud. Some people think the noise and exhaust created by snowmobiles is damaging to the environment.

Talk about the difference between noisy sounds and sounds you like. What makes a sound noisy? Create a cassette tape of a variety of everyday sounds, including those with varied volumes. Play this tape for your children. As a group, decide which sounds are noisy, and which are nice.

Snowmobile Safety

The snowmobile community annually sponsors International Snowmobile Safety Week on the third week of January. Safety manuals, brochures, decals, posters, and safety videos can be obtained through the International Snowmobile Manufacturers Association or your local snowmobile club. These clubs and organizations can be a great resource not only for materials about snowmobiles, but also for safe riding talks and demonstrations. Perhaps an instructor could bring a real snowmobile to your classroom for your children to explore.

Hint: The International Snowmobile Manufacturers Association (ISMA) can be reached at the following address: 1640 Haslett Road
Suite 170
Haslett, MI 48840
Website: www.snowmobile.org.

Mini-Snowplows

A snowplow is usually a plow blade mounted on the front end of a truck or tractor. Some blades can scoop up snow and carry it off of parking lots and other surfaces, while others scrape a path along roads and highways, letting the snow build up on either side. During months without snow, most snowplow blades can be taken off so that the truck or tractor can be used for other work.

Help your children transform toy trucks into mini-snowplows. Tear off strips of duct tape and roll them sticky-side out. Use the tape rolls to attach recipe cards to the front end of the trucks (you may need to trim the cards a little, depending on the size of the toy). Have the children use their plows for snowplow play in the sandbox or sensory table.

Variation: Fill a sensory tub with salt. Have the children pretend their fingers are snowplow blades. Encourage the children to "plow" numbers, letters, and designs in the salt "snow."

Snowplow Snack

Make a dip by mixing ranch dressing with plain yogurt, nonfat sour cream, or instant mashed potatoes. Give each of your children a dollop of dip on a paper plate. Set out square-shaped crackers and have the children pretend that the crackers are snowplow blades. They will enjoy plowing into the dip.

Variation: Substitute raw vegetables for crackers.

Plowed Over

Have your children lie on the floor with their hands to their sides. Invite them to pretend they are snowflakes that are covering the ground. Hold up one end of a rectangular piece of cardboard or posterboard for a snowplow blade. Have another adult hold up the other end. Invite the children to roll their bodies across the floor as you use the blade to gently push the "snowflakes."

Snowplow Science

Snowplow drivers sometimes drop salt or other materials onto the road behind the plow so that the remaining snow or ice will melt quickly. Set out a tray of ice cubes in front of your children. Provide them with bowls of sand, cornmeal, table salt, sea salt, and black pepper. Have the children sprinkle a different type of material onto all but one or two of the cubes in the tray. Leave the tray out on a table and check it every ten minutes. Do the plain cubes melt at the same rate as the sprinkled ones? Which materials make the ice melt faster?

Snow Removal

Talk with your children about other ways we remove snow from our cars, driveways, and roads, such as by using snow blowers, shovels, and ice scrapers. If you wish, bring these items into your classroom for your children to explore. What else could they use to remove snow?

Extension: Bury toy cars and trucks in wet sand. Have the children use plastic shovels and ice scrapers to dig them out.

Snow Skis & Snowshoes

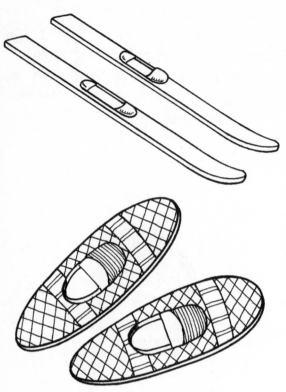

Narrow and Round

Snow skis are narrow like the runners on a sled. They are used to glide across the snow. Their shape helps people move themselves very quickly over the snow or down hills. Snowshoes are rounded. They are used to walk on top of heavy snow. Their oval shape helps to spread weight evenly so a person wearing them won't sink down into the snow.

Throughout the day, encourage your children to point out items around your room that are narrow, oval, or round. Have them guess why this is a good shape for each item.

Extension: If possible, bring in a pair of skis and a pair of snowshoes for your children to examine.

Snow Travel Song

Sung to: "Row, Row, Row Your Boat"

Swish, swish down the hill

With a happy grin.

Up, up, up the lift—

Ski back down again.

Crunch, crunch, watch me walk

Across the snowy ground.

I am wearing snowshoes

To keep from sinking down.

Have the children act out the motions as they sing this song. Encourage them to pretend to ski in the first verse, and stomp around on snowshoes in the second.

Jean Warren

Ski Moves

Show your children pictures of downhill skiers. Point out how some skiers keep their ankles together as they sway from side to side. Others control how fast they go by pointing their toes toward each other. Show them how skiers move their poles from front to back to keep steady and help them push off. Have your children put on their boots, scarves, hats, and gloves. Then sing the following song. Encourage the children to move their feet and arms as they pretend to ski.

Variation: In some free-style downhill skiing competitions, skiiers choreograph jumps, spins, and glides to music. Play some lively music and have your children pretend to jump, spin, and glide on skis.

Downhill Skiing
Sung to: "This Old Man"

Side to side,

Side to side,
  (Sway from side to side.)

Bend my knees and glide, glide, glide.
  *(Bend your knees and put hands on your
  waist as if holding up ski poles.)*

When I ski down the hill

It gives me such a thrill.

I'm careful not to take a spill.
  (All fall down.)

Carol Gnojewski

Ski Tracks

Set out dark construction paper, white paint, and craft sticks. Place a glob of white paint in the middle of each child's paper. Have your children pretend the sticks are skis. Let them move the paint across the paper using their skis to make tracks in the paint "snow."

Variation: Provide your children with a box of miscellaneous craft items. Invite them to use these items to make other tracks in the snow.

Ski Balance

Skiers and snowshoers use poles to help them keep their balance. Bring in two real ski poles. (Or use two gift-wrap tubes of identical length.) Show your children how to walk while balancing on these poles.

Extension: Talk about canes, walkers, and walking sticks, which are all used to help people keep their balance.

Ski Lifts

A ski lift is a moving belt that carries skiers to the top of a mountain trail or slope. A ski lift can have a bar, called a *tow bar* or a *T-bar*, that skiers hold onto as they are pulled up the slope; suspended chairs that skiers sit on; or a gondola, an enclosed car that skiers ride in.

After discussing tow bar, chair, and gondola lifts with your children, ask if they'd like to build one. Have them decide which type of lift they would prefer to make. Then string a cable between two bookcases or chairs in your room. Put small plastic rings on the cable, such as shower curtain rings. Let the children attach toys to the rings with yarn or wire. They will have fun moving the toys across the wire.

Ski Gondola

Provide each of your children with a ½-inch piece of drinking straw and half of a paper towel tube. Have them tape the straw to the top of the tube (or use a hot-glue gun to attach it for them, as shown in the illustration). Make sure they tape it in the middle of the tube for balance. Then let the children draw windows on the tube and decorate the outside of it as desired. Help each child string a long piece of yarn through their gondola and suspend the yarn between two bookcases or chairs, as in the Ski Lift activity. Place a small plastic animal or doll inside and let the children take it for a ride.

Variation: Invite the children to cut pictures of people out of magazines to glue onto their gondola windows for passengers.

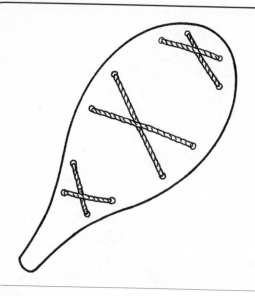

Snowshoe Lacing

Use the pattern on page 278 to make a cardboard snowshoe stencil. Provide your children with heavy paper, markers, and scissors, and help them trace and cut out the stencil. Then punch holes all around the edge of each snowshoe with a hole punch. Attach a long piece of yarn to one of the holes on each stencil, and have the children use the yarn to lace their snowshoes. Before they lace, show the children pictures of real snowshoes. Encourage them to crisscross the yarn to imitate their woven lacing pattern.

Snow Sifting

Traditionally, snowshoes were woven like baskets, The loose weaving allows the snow to sift through the shoes as you walk. This helps you stay on top of the snow.

Set out small wicker baskets (such as those used to hold paper plates for picnics) and plastic sieves. Have your children use the baskets and sieves to sift sand or salt in your sensory table.

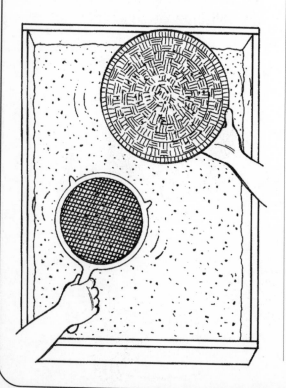

Snowshoe March

If you wish, have each of your children make two snowshoes. After they are finished lacing, attach an additional piece of yarn as a binding on either side of the snowshoes with tape or staples. Help the children tie the shoes to their feet using the yarn binding pieces. Let them practice walking and marching around the room in their snowshoes. Make sure that the handlelike tail is in the back.

Ski Sort

Paint or use markers to color six pairs of craft sticks to make skis. Make each pair a different color. Mix up the "skis" and have the children take turns sorting them.

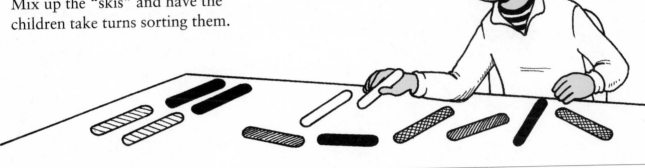

Cozy Place

After an exciting day on the slopes, most skiers stop at a ski lodge. Ski lodges are cozy buildings where skiers can rest by a fire, have a snack or warm drink, and listen to people discuss their ski adventures. Let your children talk about their favorite cozy places. What makes them cozy? Then let them help you create a cozy space in your room. Perhaps they'll want to build a pretend fire, or move all of the blankets and comfy chairs to that area. If you wish, serve a snack of hot cocoa in your cozy place. Cuddle together and tell your children a cozy wintry folktale, such as *The Mitten,* by Jan Brett (Putnam Publishing Group, 1996).

"S" Is for Snow

Make use of all the *S*-words in this unit to reinforce the letter *S* and its beginning sound. Have your children help you make a list of all of the *S*-words you have talked about, such as snow, skis, snowshoes, sift, spill, sway, slope, and swish.

Snow
skis
snowshoes
sift
spill
sway
slope
swish

Snowshoe Lacing Pattern

Use with the activity on page 276.

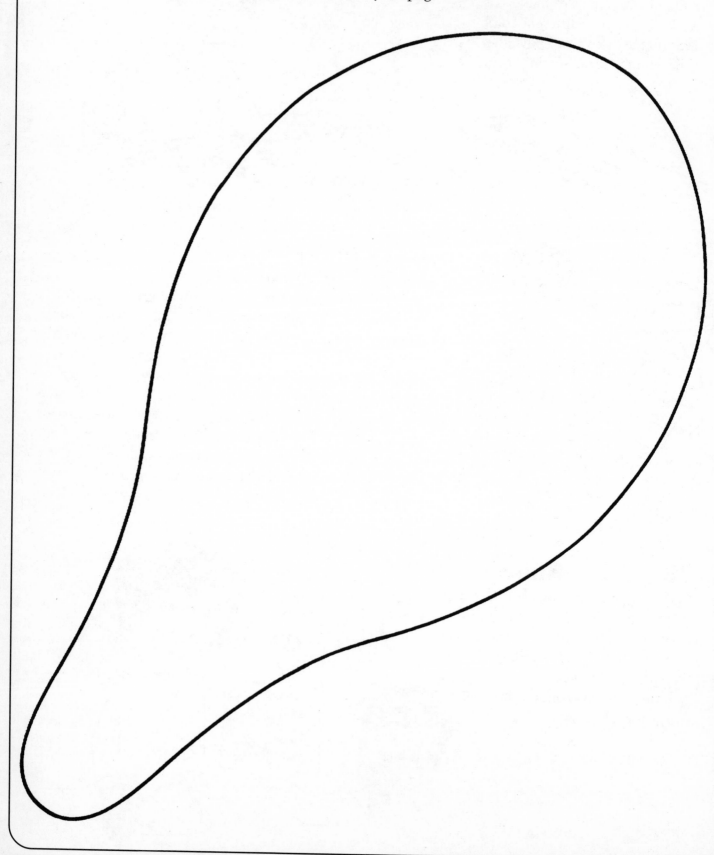